F. E. Vaughan

The Albemarle Section of North Carolina

Traversed by the Norfolk Southern Railroad

F. E. Vaughan

The Albemarle Section of North Carolina
Traversed by the Norfolk Southern Railroad

ISBN/EAN: 9783337212063

Printed in Europe, USA, Canada, Australia, Japan

Cover: Foto ©Andreas Hilbeck / pixelio.de

More available books at **www.hansebooks.com**

THE

ALBEMARLE SECTION

OF

NORTH CAROLINA

TRAVERSED BY

THE NORFOLK SOUTHERN RAILROAD

AND ITS

CONNECTING STEAMBOAT LINES.

NEW YORK:

JOHN C. RANKIN, JR., PRINTER, 34 CORTLANDT STREET.

1884.

THE ALBEMARLE SECTION.

INTRODUCTORY.

North Carolina, with a history running back as far as the year 1584—within a century of the date of the discovery of the New World by Christopher Columbus! North Carolina with its grand area of 50,000 square miles, including mountain, valley and plain, with its every variety of soil, with its forests of valuable timber, with its broad sounds and its hundred rivers navigable far inland and teeming with the choicest varieties of fish ; with its wealth of metals and minerals, and with its salubrious climate, has, strange to say, until within a comparatively recent period, been next to unknown by the busy world around it. Along its 300 miles of Atlantic coast sailed the fleets of the adventurous discoverers of the olden time ; through its sounds, with their white wings spread to the breeze, were wafted the quaint vessels of Sir Walter Raleigh. On Roanoke Island was born Virginia Dare, the first person born in America of European parentage. For North Carolina the great philosopher, Bacon, prepared the constitution of his ideal empire of perfect government. Within her borders North Carolina's sturdy sons met together and were first to declare to the world that America is and shall be free ; and the blood of those brave men was freely shed in the trying struggle that followed that declaration, in defence of honor and of home.

And yet, what of North Carolina at this day! Upon an honest and candid inquiry into the causes of the present condition of this State, and why she has but recently started from lethargy, the following explanation may be accepted.

In ante-bellum days, when slavery was a recognized institution—when the wealthy planters owned and controlled the laborers on his broad acres—the prevalence of ignorance to a great extent was a natural consequence ; not only to the slaves, but to those of the white race whose poverty compelled them to compete with slave labor. True, in those days, there were one or two colleges in the State, and quite a number of schools of lower grade ; but these, owing to the then existing state of affairs, were of advantage chiefly to the sons of the more wealthy. What, in such a state of things, was there to excite ambition, and what the inducements to press forward in the march of the world's civilization ?

The vast stores of minerals and metal were then, as now, hid away in the mountains of the State ; but then the possessors of capital had quite another use for their surplus funds than to purchase expensive machinery and undertake to develope the State's mineral wealth ; and, besides, there was really no desire to experiment in untried fields, or to engage in enterprises other than such as related to the cultivation of the lands ; the universal rule being *well enough will do*. The forests were, as now, rich in valuable timbers, but these were regarded as of but little value except for farm uses at home. The sounds and rivers were then, as now, full of excellent fish ; yet fishing was an industry of a third or fourth rate ; it was followed mainly to the extent of obtaining supplies for home use with but a few exceptions.

Agriculture was the leading and almost the only pursuit, corn, cotton, rice and tobacco, were produced in immense quantities, and, as a rule, all surplus capital, as soon as it came to hand, was invested in the purchase of land and slaves. And even the public treasury had but little that could be applied to the establishment of schools and to works of improvement, and all this tells the secret of the non-progression of a great State.

But from the necessities of the case a new regime has been adopted since the close of the late war.

The colored man is free and a citizen, and has to provide for himself, and this he may well do, for he is protected by State laws in all his rights of citizenship, and in every way encouraged to better his condition and raise himself to a higher one.

He sits on juries and votes; he has his own churches and schools. The property and polls of the State are annually taxed for the support of public schools, and the colored man gets his equal share of the fund raised, and of the school-houses and teachers with the white man, and already the more industrious of the colored race have, with these advantages, been enabled to accumulate sufficient to purchase small farms out of the broad domains of their former masters, and both races are manifestly benefited by the change. The great farms have been divided and re-divided, until, in many cases, a score of small farms have taken the place of one, and where one man raised 100 bales of cotton or 1,000 barrels of corn. twenty men now raise on the same land 150 bales of cotton and 1,500 barrels of corn. And here is positive evidence of advance that can but continue in ever increasing progression.

In ante-bellum days a State or County fair or other exhibition of natural wealth of the State, or the results of industry were almost unheard of occurrences ; but recently both County and State fairs are not only the order of the day, but they are admited to result in great profit to the people.

And yet North Carolina is not as fully awake to the advantages of such public exhibitions as she will be. and especially does this apply to the eastern part of the State. At the recent exposition at Atlanta, this State took its first forward step in the right direction by endeavoring to acquaint the world with her boundless natural wealth, and with the products of her people's industry.

At the more recent exposition at Boston she appeared again, and even to better advantage than at Atlanta. And that her exhibit at Boston was a decided success none will deny. Other States that were represented at these great fairs looked with pleasure and surprise on the exhibit made by North Carolina, and learned much of her grand resources and of the state and scope of her leading industries that they had never before known, and already immense profit to her has been the result.

GENERAL DESCRIPTION.

It is proposed to present a concise description of that part of the "Albemarle Section" of North Carolina consisting of the Counties of Carrituck, Camden, Pasquotank, Perquimans, Chowan, Dare, Tyrrell, Washington, Hyde, Bertie and Martin, eleven counties, with an area of 3,770 square miles and a population, according to the census of 1880, of 94,505—and to say something of its location as a part of the State, and of its general physical characteristics and natural features, of its soil, its farms, forests and flora, its towns and villages, its agricultural productions, of its commercial location and advantages as regards the markets of the world, its climate, its schools, its railroads and modes and conveniences of travel and transportation of freights, of the usual modes of farming, average yield of lands and pieces of lands, of labor, and of the reasonable inducements it presents for the profitable investment of capital, and for the emigrant from other States or from foreign lands to make it his home.

It will be seen by a glance at the map that the eleven counties mentioned form one contiguous body in the extreme north-eastern portion of the State, bounded by Virginia on the north, and the Atlantic Ocean on the east, and by about the latitude of Cape Hatteras on the south. In this territory are the whole of Currituck, Albemarle, Roanoke and Croatan Sounds, and the large part of Pamlico Sound. Its chief navigable rivers are North, Pasquotauk, Little, Perquimans, Yeopim, Chowan, Cashie, Roanoke, Scuppernong, Alligator, Long Shoal, Pamlico, Pungo and Tar. Within it are Lake Mattamuskeet and Lake Scuppernong, and many creeks that empty into the rivers and sounds. The country is

level, with an average elevation of about fifteen to twenty
feet above the sea. That portion of the sea beach callèd
" Banks," within this territory, is about 100 miles long,
with an average width of one mile. Roanoke Island, the
largest island in the territory, is about twelve miles long
by two wide. Knott's Island, Crow Island and Churches
Island, in Currituck Sound, are noted centres for the
hunter of wild fowl. Most of the sounds and rivers and
some of the creeks are navigable far inland for vessels of
large class. About one-half of the whole area of 3,770
square miles is at this day cleared and under cultivation,
and about 1,000 square miles are still covered by virgin
forest.

Of the 1,800 square miles, more or less of forest lands,
at least 1,500 are susceptible of cultivation, leaving in
the territory 300 square miles that can not be used for
farm purposes except after great expense of dyking and
draining. The general character of the soil of the section is a sandy loam, with here and there yellow and gray
clay, but the " banks " are throughout of a yellow glossy
sand, in many places constantly drifting, and, for the
most part, utterly lacking in vegetation, although at
places are tracks of stunted woodland where their accu-
mulations of vegetable matter mingles with the soil, and
at such places grapes, figs, melons and potatoes are cultivated with considerable profit. But little attention is
given to the cultivation of these sands, the chief and
almost only occupation of the " banker " being fishing
and fowling. Throughout the entire length of the banks
is a government telegraph line, and all along, at a distance of five miles apart, are life saving stations, and at
intervals of twenty miles or so a great light-house con-
structed of stone and brick is seen steepling up hundreds
of feet in the air. The islands of the sounds have, generally, enough of vegetable matter mixed with the sands
to render them very productive, and some of them
throughout their whole extent are gardens of beauty,
with here and there clumps and hammocks of trees and
patches of corn and melons, and vineyards and orchids,
and flower fringed creeks and bays.

The mainland of the district, to wit: that part of it lying west of Currituck, Croatan and Pamlico Sounds, has in the composition of its soil much less of sand and more of clay throughout, but certain localities have far more of clay or of sand than other localities. The clay soils are "stiff" in proportion to the greater or less quantity of clay mixed with the sand ; the more sandy lands are easier of tillage and are less injuriously affected by extremes of dry and wet weather than the "stiff" lands, and they are on this account, as well as that the "loose" lands can be more cheaply cultivated, preferred by the farmer. There are strata of white sand, gravel, blue clay, marl, etc., underlying much of the lands both stiff and loose.

The wells of water in this whole region are shallow, and generally extend to no greater depth than the stratum of white sand from which spring abundance of clear water. In some of the more eastern counties are large areas—in some instances 50,000 acres in a body—of land known as "swamp land." There is something peculiar in these swamp lands—they are generally higher than the surrounding country, and are therefore easy of drainage and susceptible of cultivation. One of these tracts—a branch of the Great Dismal Swamp—has its summit nearly in its centre. This summit or greatest elevation is a ridge extending its whole length, from which the water shed is in opposite direction. A ditch recently cut from a creek, three miles back into the swamp, has a fall of eight feet in that distance which pours the water down in a torrent.

Lake Drummond, at about the centre of the Dismal Swamp, has a general depth of about ten feet ; the surface of this lake is about on a level with the tops of the windows of the second stories of houses in Norfolk. The bottom of the lake is full fifteen feet above the streets of Norfolk.

The explanation of the anomaly is that the "swamp" is literally covered and matted with rank vegetation that prevents the running off of the waters that fall on it, and they are so held until they can evaporate and ooze through the sandy loam to the lower level of the rivers, on account of which slow process of draining the lands are almost continually wet, and hence are known as swamps.

No doubt these swamps would long ago have been converted into farms but for the expense of clearing and ditching them by a sparse population with abundance of other lands at hand more cheaply and easily brought into a state of cultivation. But large tracts of these swamps have been brought into cultivation and have proved to be the very best and most productive and valuable lands in the district, notably, the splendid plantation of 2,400 acres in Pasquotank County, belonging to Mr. George W. Sanderlin, the "Tadmore" farms in the same county, of Messrs. J. R. Etheridge, A. F. Stafford, W. C. Foster and others, the farms of Messrs. C. L. Pettigrew and Herbert H. Page and others in Washington County, and those of Col. W. S. Carter and others near "Mattamuskeet" Lake, in Hyde County. Some of these farms have produced, in exceptionally favorable seasons, as much as 120 bushels of corn to the acre without the application of manure, and as much as 66 bushels of rice to the acre. There is no better region for the growth of the hay grasses, and as much as four tons of red clover and timothy have been raised on an acre. On these swamps grow vast fields of reeds, affording abundant pasturage for cattle through the spring, summer, fall and part of the winter. The top earth of the rich lands mentioned is a dark alluvium to the depth sometimes of two feet, based upon a stratum of sand and pebbles. or upon marl from two to four feet deep, beneath which comes generally tough blue clay and then white sand.

On these swamp tracts grow vast quantities of timber of several kinds, but chiefly cypress and black gum and poplar, and maple on the deepest soils, pine on the stiffest and poorest sections, and juniper on the peety lands. The juniper generally appears in thickets or "greens," covering tracts of a half acre to 100 acres, or even more. This timber is in great demand for cooper logs, shingles, railroad ties, etc., and is cut and shipped to markets out of the State in large quantities.

Another thing may here be said in connection with
these "greens".: The water springs that bubble up at
places through the peat is of a dark reddish color and is
remarkably clear and healthful, owing in some degrees; it
is said, to the tannic acid it contains, and will keep for
years without bilging or becoming in the least stagnant.
Some of it was experimented with to test its qualities in
this particular, by the United States Government before
the late war. Large tanks were filled with it and put into
the receiving ship "Pennsylvania" at Portsmouth, Va.
After it had been in the tanks more than twenty years it
was tested and found to be as pure and sweet as when
put in, the only change in it was that it had lost its
color and became as clear as crystal.

U. S. Vessels bound upon long cruises are now supplied with "juniper water." No instance is on record
of the juniper swamp hands being at any time troubled
with malaria in any form while they drank this water.

The "highlands" of the district, as all except the
"swamps" are called by way of distinguishing them, as
has been said, are the stiff and loose lands. The stiff
lands are best adapted to the cultivation of wheat and
corn and fruits of some kinds. The loose lands produce
good corn, but are not adapted to wheat. On these lands
the staples are cotton, peas, peanuts, sweet and Irish
potatoes, melons, strawberries, grapes, and trucks of
many varieties, but the best cotton land is a grayish
sandy clay.

Rice, the grasses and oats are best produced on the
deep alluvial soils. The most valuable timber on the
highlands is pine, of which there are vast quantities
throughout the entire district; in some localities are
quantities of oak and maple, in others ash, maple of several varieties, gum of several varieties, holly, dogwood, etc.

The flora of this region is not surpassed in beauty,
variety and luxuriance by any other section of the State.
At one season yellow jassamine, crimson woodbine and
the pure white dogwood predominate, filling the whole
air with their perfumes. At another wild roses, wild

cotton, and the scarlet leaves of the maple picture the forests and the river borders with beautiful tints, and at all times during the spring, summer and autumn a thousand varieties individually less conspicuous than those mentioned carpet wood and field with their myriad beautiful faces.

With all the natural advantages the Albemarle Section, strange to say, has slowly recuperated from the destroying effects of the late war.

A new era has dawned and a new departure for better things is already so plainly apparent that he who runs may read the glad tidings of the nearing of a brighter day. And of the truth of the assertion that *advance* is now the watch-word, the intelligent reader will require no further proof than to know the facts following, briefly stated.

There are double the number of school-houses that there were twenty years ago, presided over by carefully selected, competent teachers. An excellent public free school system is supplied with twice the amount of funds of former days. The school-houses are more comfortably and conveniently arranged, and the text books uniform. There are twice the number of private schools, whose teachers are continually learning and adopting the improved methods of teaching. An increasing number of intelligent farmers are giving attention to the science of chemistry, adopting the most improved farm utensils and machinery, and are listing farming among the sciences. They are putting their farms in order by draining them, fencing them well, improving the dwelling and out-houses, taking pains with their teams and stock, experimenting with the different manures and commercial fertilizers, studying the character of the soils, and the diversity and rotation of crops. Our fisheries are being operated on improved plans, the seines are laid out and drawn in by steam, and as a consequence five hauls of a seine can be made now in the same time that three were made formerly.

There is a very much greater diversity of the industries, there being five manufactories now for one in the year

1860. And these are but a few of the gleams that augur the coming of a bright morning.

And now, one word in addition to the preceding general statements; no fairer field for the profitable investment of capital presents itself in the whole extent of the country. Nor can the emigrant find a better place for his permanent home. Is the farmer in search of lands that are both productive and cheap? Here he will find good lands that he can purchase at ten dollars per acre, or less. Is the mechanic on the look out for work at remunerative wages, and pleasant home for his family? He can rest at no better place, or one with a more hopeful future in view. Is the American manufacturer, who has been operating in New England, and North and West, in overworked fields, casting about for new and more profitable fields? He will surely find them here. From 50,000 to 75,000 bales of cotton pass through Elizabeth City alone, yearly, on their way to the manufacturer. Why should not a large portion of this be manufactured before moving? Certainly the great Wendell Philips was not mistaken when he said in substance, the manufacturer is wise who moves his machinery to the cotton field instead of waiting for the cotton to be moved from the field to the machinery. There are many opportunities of profitable investment in various directions in the Albermarle district that the observant capitalist cannot fail to see and appreciate if he will but look.

HISTORICAL.

The Albermarle section first became known to the civilized world in July, 1584, probably about the fourth day of the month, according to the computation of the new style. Its new birth into the family of civilized people was under most auspicious influences and circumstances. The illustrious Queen Elizabeth, most renowned of English potentates, was upon the throne, and Sir Walter Raleigh, the most illustrious Englishman of his time—illustrious in arms, in letters, in enterprise, in gallantry, in learning, and as the man who first introduced to the civilized world the commerce and use of tobacco, that has built up colossal fortunes in factory and field, that is one of the most remedial agents known to the Materia Medica, that has been a solace and a comfort to age and manhood, and that is the recognized symbol of good will throughout the world, both savage and civilized, wherever man has smoked the calumet of peace, stood sponsor for it at the baptismal font of nations. In April, 1584, Sir Walter Raliegh obtained a patent from Queen Elizabeth and fitted out two ships, under Captains Philip Amidas and Arthur Barlow, which sailed from England and landed in July on Roanoke Island, in the lower Albemarle Sound. First returning thanks to Almighty God, for protecting them in their perilous voyage, Amidas took formal possession of the country in "the name of Elizabeth of England as rightful Queen and Princess of the same." Amidas, in his report of the discovery described it as a "goodlie land, the fragrance of which, as they drew near the land, was as if they had been in the midst of some delicate garden, abounding in all manner of odoriferous flowers." The hardy mariners were delighted with the natives and with the country. The Indians were kind, hospitable and generous, and Amidas and Barlow, after a short stay, returned to England in September, taking with them two Indians, and creating a thrilling interest throughout England by descriptions of the country and its inhabitants. To give greater eclat to the discovery which had been made by Sir Walter's captains, the Queen named the country Virginia after herself, a Virgin queen. Public curiosity was excited to see the new country and the strange people who were without guile, and in which the manners were like the "golden age." The spirit of adventure and the thirst for discovery was aroused, and there was no difficulty in enlisting new adventurers for a second expedition to Roanoke Island. On the 19th of April, 1585, Sir Walter Raliegh fitted out and dispatched a colony with Sir Ralph Lane as Governor, and they landed on Roanoke Island again in July. They remained about a year, but not effecting a permanent location, they returned to England dissatisfied under the hardship and sacrifices incident to their adventurous life. Soon after their departure a ship loaded with every comfort came out from Sir Walter, and was joined by three other ships commanded by Sir Richard Greenville, but they sought the colony in vain that was brought out by Lane. After a fruitless search they returned, leaving fifteen men on the Island. In January of the next year, 1587, a third colony, more fully fitted out, furnished and equipped, was sent out by Sir Walter under command of John White, who was commissioned as "Governor of the City of Raleigh." They, too, arrived in July. This colony of White's was accompanied by women and children, and their purpose was to make a permanent settlement and a new home. He was accompanied by his daughter, Eleanor Dare ; and his grand-daughter, Virginia Dare, named in compliment to England's queen, was the *first born* of English parents in the new land. The fifteen men left by Sir Richard Greenville could not be found. But White's colony was not dispirited. They laid the foundations of the City of Raleigh on Roanoke Island, the remains of which still exist. They builded, they planted, they worshipped God, reared the altars of the Church of England, and admitted to the Communion of the Church the

Indian Manteo, by baptism. The grape and fig tree grew
spontaneously around them, the earth yielded its increase,
and it seemed indeed a goodly heritage. But strife with
the Indians succeeded the hospitality of their first coming. That irrepressible conflict of race which, commenc-
ing then has gone on ever, soon arose and checked the
happiness of the colony. White returned to England for
assistance, leaving a colony on the island of eighty-nine
men, seventeen women and two children. It was agreed
that if the remnant of the colony should be compelled by
any circumstances to leave Roanoke Island, the place to
which they should go was to be designated, and if distress overtook them they should indicate it by a cross.
Upon his return to England White found the country
involved in war with Spain, the rival in arms of England.
Public attention was diverted from the infant colony, and
it was more than two years before he could return to
Roanoke. He came at last, but could find nothing of the
colony. He searched for some vestiges of them and
found upon the shore, near the site of their settlement, a
post with the word *Croatan* carved upon it. No sign of
distress was carved near it; no trace, no authentic tradition, no reliable statement, no memento of that lost
colony exists or has ever been found. The Indians knew
nothing or would tell nothing of them. They passed
away without mark or memorial, and will ever remain
the lost link in the history of the Albemarle section.
After this ineffectual attempt to make a permanent settlement on Roanoke Island, the spirit of adventure and discovery was diverted to Virginia, entering in at Chespeake
Bay. And after hardships and imminent abandonment
permanent settlements were effected on James River:
they were, however, all the legitimate offsprings
of Sir Walter Raleigh's enterprise on Roanoke Island,
the germ and fruit of the seed then planted. The next
ingress of settlers in the Albemarle section came from the
James river country of Virginia; the population of that
section first coming over into the country on Nansemond
River, and thence extending into the adjacent sections
along Chowan and Roanoke rivers. It was in July,

again, in 1653, sixty-nine years after Amidas and Barlow had landed on Roanoke Island, that settlements along the upper Albemarle Sound first began to attract attention. They were probably not organized colonists, but trappers, hunters and others, attracted by a life of wild adventures, and in some cases, perhaps, fugitives from the restraints of law and order. They probably banded together in considerable numbers for protection against savages and had no government among themselves except voluntary association and rude justice summarily administered. One Roger Green, of whose character and achievements history has failed to preserve any memorials, appears to have been the most conspicuous of these adventurers. Some refugees from religious persecutions, the fruitful source of our early settlements, had preceded him.

But the year 1662 may be put down as the date of the first organized permanent settlement in the Albemarle Section and George Durant, a Quaker broad-brim, as the proto-pioneer and permanent settler. Old George was of a genuine type of Friends ; careful, pains-taking, unostentatious, thrifty. obstinate, and fair in his dealings. He bought lands on Albemarle Sound in what was afterward called Durant's Neck in Perquimans County, bought them of Kuscatenew, "King of the Yeopim Indians," paid for them fairly, and the deed is on record in Perquimans County, the oldest deed in North Carolina, the original of which on vellum was long in possession of Gen. J. H. Jacock, of Perquimans, who owned part of the original Geo. Durant tract. The deed is probably yet in the possession of Gen. Jacock's descendants. For a long time in the early history of the Albermarle Section government was very irregular. The Quaker element was large and the religious sentiment was divided between them and the communion of the Church of England. The latter had the authority from the home government and unquestionably exercised a severe rule over those dissenting in religious faith. Bitter feeling always prevailed and sometimes violent outbreaks, civic feuds and bloody contests. The dark and bloody history of

Cary's rebellion, in which for years the colony was torn with the clash of contending arms, the peace disturbed and the public records destroyed ; all grew out of this religious contest between those who professed to follow in the footsteps of the meek and lowly "Prince of peace."

The bloody struggles with the Indians are conspicuous in the early proprietory government of the Albermarle Section. About 1711 a general massacre of the white settlers, concerted and planned with great secrecy, was partially carried out. On the Roanoke and Chowan Rivers, in the counties of Bertie and Hertford, many fell by the murderous savage hand. It was suppressed, after imminent danger of entire extermination, with the assistance of our kind brothers from South Carolina. Omitting many interesting portions of Albemarle history our brief space brings us to the revolutionary period. In that time of trial Albemarle did its whole duty. The vestry of old St. Paul's Church of Edenton were hardly behind the heroes of Mecklenburg in their opposition to the unrepresented taxation of Great Britan, and, when peaceful but indignant protests were followed by sanguinary conflicts, her sons were not slow to buckle on their armor and lead or follow where duty called. And when the sword was sheathed and the soldiers arms were moulded into plow shares, she brought to the civil service of the country a fidelity and force that would do honor to any country. Peace brought prosperity and prosperity brought elegance and cultured refinement; the Albemarle country was a blooming rose-bed of beauty, with rich farms, teeming fields, and a proud race of baronial planters, dispensing liberal and elegant hospitality and happiness all around them. Cruel war came again, civil war, intensifying the horrors of all wars, and all was changed, and the day of recovery is just beginning.

CLIMATE. *

By reference to the mean parallels of latitude of the United States it will be seen that North Carolina is situated nearly midway of the Union; and inasmuch as those States lie entirely within the temperate zone, it follows that North Carolina is situated upon the central belt of that zone. This position gives to the State a climate not excelled by any in the world. She is exempt from the extreme cold which prevails in the Northern States, and to a considerable extent from the early frosts which visit the States immediately north of her, on the one hand ; and from the torrid heat and malarial influnces which prevail in the States to the south of her on the other. Other causes apart from its position concur to produce this result. On the west the lofty Appalachian chain interposes its mighty barrier between the bleak winds of the north-west and the general surface of the State. On the east the coast is swept by the Gulf Stream, the meliorating effect of which is felt far inland. From these causes combined the temperature of the seasons ranges within moderate limits. The spring comes in with less of those fickle variations which mark its advent elsewhere on this continent. The summers are not oppressive, even in the low country, or if so, for a few days only. But in the autumn nature here exhibits herself in her most benignant mood in her most favored zone. From the incoming of October to the latter part of December there is an almost uninterrupted succession of bright, sunny days, during which the air is dry, crisp and pure —a season equally favorable to the ingathering of the crops and to active exertion of every kind. The reign of

winter as respects cold and wet is short, and field labor
is carried on throughout that season, with the exception
of two or three days at a time. Frost makes its appearance
about the fifteenth of October, and sometimes, there is not
enough to nip the tender vegetation until the end of No-
vember. From the Blue Ridge to the seaboard, ice rarely
forms of a thickness to be gathered except in localities
overhung and deeply shaded by high southern bluffs.
When snow falls it covers the ground for only a few
inches, and is quickly dissipated by the sun. Fogs are
of rare occurance, and then mainly in the form of a belt
of light vapor marking the course of the larger streams in
the latter part of summer and during the autumn months.
The average rainfall throughout the State is fifty-three
inches, which is pretty uniformly distributed through
the year.

Dr. Kerr, in his Geological Report, classes the climate
of the different sections of North Carolina, with reference
to their isothermal ranges, as follows: "Middle and
eastern North Carolina correspond to middle and southern France, and western North Carolina to northern France
and Belgium. And all the climates of Italy, from Palermo
to Milan and Venice, are represented."

Very erroneous impressions prevail as to the healthfulness of our climate, especially among the people of
the North. That authentic and official information on
this point might be presented, a letter was addressed to
Dr. S. S. Satchwell, President of the North Carolina
State Board of Health, from whose reply the following
extract is made:

"The labors of the board in the great cause of sanitary
improvement and of preventive medicine, have already
enabled us to arrive at very gratifying results for our
State as bearing upon its sickness and mortality. There
are few regions of the whole earth where the conditions
of climate are more favorable to health, human comfort,
and physical well-being than are the climatic conditions
of North Carolina, leaving out as exceptions certain cir-
cumscribed local regions where malaria is liable to exist
at certain seasons. There is not a more delightful

climate for pleasure or health than that of North Carolina. It is not excelled by the most favored climatic conditions of Italy or France. The climate of the *eastern* and middle portions of our State correspond to that of the middle and south of France, and that of western North Carolina to that of the north of France and Belgium—regions noted the world over for the geniality and healthfulness of their climate. The splendid climates of Italy from Palermo to Milan and Venice, are correctly represented in those of our own salubrious and health-giving State. Nor are the topographical features and geological structures of the State, so generally favorable to ready and efficient drainage—always a prime element of health—less adapted to the production of the low rate of sickness and of death that prevails in North Carolina, outside of those localities of malaria, alluded to as less salubrious, and which, under the increasing application and dominion of the spade, axe and hoe, are steadily becoming more and more healthy as cultivation increases. So far as that prevalent and fatal scourge, consumption, is concerned, it has been found that one of the two small areas of total exemption in the whole country from this dread destroyer of the human race, is found in North Carolina. Nature, whether in the magnificence and wealth of our climate ; the fertility and adaptation of the soils as well as climate to the production of the various industries that are most conducive to the prosperity of the people and the wellfare of the State ; or in the vast wealth of the underlying geological structures of the State, everywhere asserts, as statistics prove, that there is no State in the Union more healthy than North Carolina. With the natural conditions of insalubrity existing only in a local and exceptional degree, and giving way, as they will, before the great work of removal of preventable causes and preventable diseases, now happily inaugurated in North Carolina, by State authority, in the organization by the last Legislature of a State Board of Health, we can but cherish a lively and reasonable hope that the average rate of sickness and mortality will steadily decrease under the operation of

the benign influence of Sanitary science. *Already it is
less than the average in the United States.* Sanitary
statistics, such as we have been able to obtain in the
prosecution of the official labors and duties assigned to
the Board, combined with other information obtained
from reports and data in our possession, justifies the assertion that sickness and death in North Carolina presents *a rate less than one per cent. against an average of
more than one and a quarter per cent.*, taking all the
States into the calculation in deducing an average
rate."

The following,*from a report to the State upon its swamp
lands, presents the substantial facts about the health of
this section : " Referring to the reports of Prof. Ebenezer
Emmons, a former State geologist, he says it may be in-
ferred that as the swamp lands are so low and wet, that
they must necessarily be extremely unhealthy, or become
so when drained and the vegetable matter begins to de-
compose.   Experience, however, does not support this
view. The testimony of those who have cultivated them
for forty years is that their families have enjoyed as
much health as their neighbors who have lived at a distance. Persons who are in the habit of plunging into the
swamp lands knee deep for draining, and, when drained,
to live in the immediate vicinity of the extended surface
of black vegetable mould for years, are rarely sick with
fevers. The points which are unhealthy are those which
are exposed to winds which blow off extended surfaces
of the waters of the Neuse and Cape Fear rivers.
Miasma, which generates fever, arises more from the
banks of rivers than from the swamp and pocoson soils."
And Gen. Blount, in a letter to Prof. Emmons, says:
"I have been for a period of forty years engaged
in reclaiming and cultivating swamp lands, such as
I have described, and have found it a profitable business.   I am located near the margin of the swamp
(of which my plantation is a part); it contains 30,000
acres, and is south of my residence. The health of my

---

* Report on the Swamp Lands, by Walter Gwinn, 1867.

family, white and black, will compare favorably with the healthiest locations in eastern North Carolina."

Mr. Ruffin* says : "From the existing condition of the land and the waters of this lake region, every stranger would infer the general and worst effects of malaria in producing disease and death. But I was assured that such was not the fact, and that the residents suffered but little from autumnal diseases. And this I could readily believe, even after making the proper allowance for the too favorable view as to health which every man takes of his own place of residence. The people I saw had the appearance of enjoying at least ordinary good health. Among the number I saw there were three neighboring resident proprietors, each of seventy or more years of age, and then in good health. Few of the residents remove to or visit the high lands in the autumn, and these few for short times, and more in pursuit of pleasure than health. Nevertheless, admitting, as I believe is true, that the lake lands are much more healthy than the low main land (and what is called the dry land) of eastern North Carolina, still much improvement even in this respect would be made here by a general system of proper drainage." I could here make a concurrent statement of my own observations and experiences during the past thirty-seven years, which would be equally as striking ; but for brevity's sake I will confine myself to a single instance, that of Mr. J. M. Franck, who has resided upwards of forty years in Onslow County, on the western border of the great White Oak Swamp, in the fork of Cahoon and Squires Creeks, which unite in his plantation just before the confluence of their combined waters with New River ; and for twenty consecutive years there was not a single case of fever on his place, and the attendance of a physician was not once required. These facts corroborate the views advanced by Dr Charles E. Johnson, in an admirable address on malaria, delivered before the Medical Society of North Car-

---

* The late Hon. Edmund Ruffin, of Virginia, in "Sketches of Lower North Carolina."

olina in 1851, and are conformable to my own experience, namely : "As Chief Engineer of the State, I was engaged in draining swamp lands in Tyrrell County from 1839 to 1843, a period of three years. The main feature of this drainage consisted in lowering Lakes Pungo and Alligator, each five feet. This was effected by cutting canals twenty-five and thirty feet wide respectively, which dried a surface of about 70,000 acres that was covered with water. Lateral canals were then cut twelve and sixteen feet wide, a mile apart. The work was done by contract, the average number of hands employed being about 250, all negroes, except the overseers and contractors. The latter were constantly exposed to the weather ; the negroes worked every day in water and muck, generally knee deep ; they, as also the overseers, were housed in shanties on the banks of the canals, and there was not a single case of fever on the work, nor was the attention of a physician required in any instance."

In building the railroads from Petersburg to Blakely, from Portsmouth to Weldon, from Weldon to Wilmington, from Wilmington to Manchester, and from Goldsboro to Raleigh, every variety of sandy soils, wet and dry, and every species of marsh, swamp and pocoson soils were encountered and upturned, yet there were but few cases of fever, and they occurred chiefly at Blakely, which was the first terminus of the Petersburg railroad on the Roanoke river, three miles below Weldon ; and on the Great Pee Dee river in South Carolina. the intermediate points were almost entirely exempt, and remarkably so in the valley of the Cape Fear river opposite Wilmington, where the Manchester road crosses Eagle's Island, through Cypress swamp and neglected rice fields. Although the men employed were chiefly foreigners, disregarding the precautions given them to keep within doors at night, often slept on the ground on the timber used in the construction of the road, yet there was not a single case of ague and fever among them, nor did any one of them lose more than two or three days during the entire period they were engaged in the work, which was in the summer and autumn of 1853 and 1854.

While on the North Carolina Railroad from Goldsboro to Charlotte, after reaching Raleigh, ague and fever was of frequent occurrence on parts of the line passing through the argillaceous soils, and was particularly severe on the dry red clay ridge in Mecklenburg County, west of Salisbury.

I am aware that these facts do not square with preconceived opinions, and cannot be explained by the popular doctrine of a specific miasma which eminates from a decomposition of vegetable matter. They prove exactly the reverse—that where poludæ effluvia might be expected it did not arise ; that malaria and the product of vegetable decomposition are two distinct things ; that the cause of fever does not emenate from vegetable putrefaction, but that exhalations from dry argillaceous soils, newly excavated, in which there is no vegetable matter, is a fruitful source of fever, and often of a virulent character, such as the typhoid fever that prevailed in Wake, west of Raleigh, in Orange and in Alamance counties, along the line of the North Carolina Railroad, during the process of grading."

The simple and ordinary precautions which any intelligent person will employ in preservation of health are efficient protection against the commonly accepted influences of this section. Plain and well prepared food, water from deep wells or cisterns, cleanliness and avoidance of night air in the autumnal months are all that is necessary.

A gentleman who lived for two years in the Albemarle Section during the construction of the Norfolk Southern Railroad, daily exposed in the open air during all seasons of the year, by the simple precaution of shielding himself from the sun, and drinking only filtered rain water, together with a plain and nutritious diet, avoided all trace of malarial influence.

The following table compiled from observation taken through a series of years will show the range, relations and general character of the climate better than description.

METEOROLOGY OF THE ALBEMARLE SECTION.

	TEMPERATURE								RAIN AND CLOUDS								HUMIDITY	
	Mean		Maximum		Minimum		Range		Rain Fall in inches		Number of Fair Days		Number of Cloudy Days		Number of Rainy Days		MEAN HUMIDITY	
	State	Albe. Sec.	State	Albe. Sec.	State	Albe. Sec.	State	Albe. Sec.	State	Albe. Sec.	State	Albe. Sec.	State	Albe. Sec.	State	Albe. Sec.	State	Albe. Sec.
January	41	44	68	72	18	21	50	51	4.5	4.9	11	11	12	11	8	7	72	64
February	43	45	69	71	19	21	50	50	5.3	5.1	7	8	15	14	9	9	69	71
March	47	48	72	73	22	24	50	49	4.0	3.8	12	13	10	9	9	9	67	69
April	56	60	82	83	37	38	45	45	3.9	3.9	11	12	10	7	8	10	66	69
May	67	69	87	88	47	51	40	37	3.9	4.5	12	12	9	8	9	8	7	69
June	75	76	91	93	60	60	31	33	4.3	4.9	10	13	8	4	9	9	72	72
July	79	80	93	93	69	72	24	21	4.9	5.9	9	11	8	6	9	10	72	76
August	77	79	92	93	61	54	31	29	6.1	7.1	10	12	10	6	10	10	76	79
September	71	73	89	91	54	56	35	35	4.5	5.8	12	13	9	6	7	7	75	82
October	59	61	81	82	34	36	47	46	3.3	3.9	17	18	6	5	4	4	74	80
November	47	49	70	72	19	23	51	49	3.4	3.5	11	14	10	8	7	7	66	72
December	40	43	65	67	15	17	50	50	3.7	3.9	10	11	14	13	10	10	73	72
Spring	57	59	87	88	22	24	65	64	12.8	13.5	35	38	30	24	27	26		
Summer	77	79	93	93	59	60	34	33	15.9	17.5	29	36	26	16	28	27		
Autumn	59	60	89	91	23	23	66	68	11.9	13.2	40	45	25	19	19	18		
Winter	41	46	69	72	15	17	54	55	13.5	13.9	28	30	43	38	27	26		
Year	59	60	93	93	15	17	78	76	53.1	58.1	132	149	134	97	101	97	70	73 Average.

AGRICULTURAL.

A comprehensive description of the extent, methods and results of general agriculture in the Albemarle section is beyond the scope and purpose of this paper. A few facts and illustrations have been collated and are presented with the expectation that to the practical agriculturist they will suggest enough to prompt him to that inquiry which is the reward sought by this effort. Throughout this entire section cotton, corn, oats, sorghum, peas, potatoes, especially sweet potatoes, and peanuts are the staple crops. Upon the rich alluvions and the reclaimed lake and swamp lands, corn, with peas planted in the intervals between the corn, forms the exclusive crop. Occasionally on the broad low-grounds of the Roanoke wheat is grown to a considerable extent. The upland variety of rice has been introduced within a few years past with entire success. The cultivation of jute also has been the subject of experiment with like success, and it only needs proper encouragement to be grown to any extent. This section is everywhere underlaid with marl—a mixture of carbonate of lime and clay formed by the decomposition of the imbedded shells—sufficient in quantity, when raised and applied to the surface, to bring it to a high pitch of fertility and maintain it so. When cleared it yields good crops of corn and cotton for a few years without manure; and always with slight help from proper commercial fertilizers. There are other extensive areas where clay enters so largely into the soil as to form a clay loam. The counties on the north side of Albemarle Sound—a very fertile tract of county—are examples of this class. The alluvial lands of this section—lands always in the highest degree productive from the

fact that all the elements of fertility are intimately inter-
mingled by having been once suspended in water—are of
unusual extent and importance. The grain grown there
supplies food not only for people of other parts of the
State, but large populations in other States. There are
other extensive areas where the shells of the Eocene era
of the Tertiary formation—and which have been decom-
posed by time—crop out to the surface and impart to
the soil a high degree of fertility. Another class of land,
in point of fertility equaling any in the world, is that reclaimed from some of the lakes of this section. To two
of these, the process of drainage has been applied, lakes
Mattamuskeet and Scuppernong. By canals dug from
the lakes to the nearest streams, affording the necessary
fall, a wide margin entirely around the lakes has been
brought into cultivation. These lands seem to be
absolutely inexhaustable. The cultivation of three-
quarters of a century has made no change in their
productive capacity. To the lands reclaimed from
the borders of marshes—so frequent near the sea
shore—the same remark may be strictly applied.
If the indications of nature are to be relied on, North
Carolina, was plainly marked out as the land for vineyards. In the sober narrative of the voyage of Amadas
and Barlowe made in 1584 to North Carolina, then an
unbroken wilderness, the author tells us: "We viewed
the land about us, being where we first landed very sandy,
and low towards the water side, but so full of grapes, as
the very beating and surge of the sea overflowed them,
of which we found such plenty as well there as in all
places else, both on the sand and on the green soil, on
the hills as in the plains, as well on every little shrub as
also climbing towards the tops of high cedars, that I think
in all the world the like abundance is not to be found;
and myself having seen those parts of Europe that most
abound, find such difference as were incredible to be
written." Upon the visit of the voyagers to the house of
the Indian King on Roanoke Island, wine was set before
them by his wife. It is further mentioned that, "while
the grape lasteth they (the Indians) drink wine;" they

had not learned the art of preserving it. Harriot, a distinguished man in an age of distinguished men, of whom
it was justly said that he cultivated all sciences and excelled in all, visited the same coast in 1586, where he was
struck with the abundance of grape vines, and he was
impressed with the fact that wine might be made one of
the future staples of the State. "Were they," he
writes, "planted and husbanded as they ought, a principal commodity of wines might be raised." This State
has proved to be far richer in this respect than it is probable even he suspected. Grape vines were found in
equal profusion in the original forest throughout the
State. They often interlaced the trees to such an extent
that they were a serious impediment to the work of clearing away the forest, catching and suspending the trees
as they were felled. At this day if a tract of forest is enclosed, and cattle of every kind excluded, they spring up
spontaneously and thickly over the land. Some of the
finest wine grapes of the United States, the Scuppernong,
the Isabella, the Catawba and the Lincoln, are native to
this State. But it was long before the bounty of nature
in this regard was improved. This was probably due to
the fact that the State was settled almost wholly by emigrants from the British isles, who knew nothing of the
culture of the vine. It was planted here and there to yield
grapes for table use ; but it was not until within thirty
years that a vineyard was known in the State. Within that
period several of large and a great number of small extent
have been planted. Grapes in season are abundantly supplied for domestic consumption, and shipped in hundreds
of tons. The wines of the established vineyards are held
in high and just repute."*

The following table, based upon reliable data obtained from the United States Census Reports, and
especially gathered from the most trustworthy private
sources, applies to the whole Albemarle Section.. The
yield per acre is a fair average of the amounts produced on the lands adapted to the cultivation of the

*Hand Book of North Carolina.

several crops specified, with the indifferent appliances in
general use. The best lands produce more largely, and,
with improved implements and a better system of agriculture, the average for all the lands would be at least
double. The cost of making the crops is meant to represent, as accurately as can be estimated by practical
farmers, all the expense of making and putting the crop
in shape for market, including the baling of cotton,
threshing of small grain, expressing the syrup from
sorghum cane, etc. The estimate does not include the
rent of land, cost of improvements on same, or use of
team and cultivating implements. Only the staple products appear in the table. There is no available data
upon which to ascertain cost of raising trucks. The number of acres cultivated by one horse vary with the character of the soil. On the stiff lands, 25 acres is called
a one-horse crop ; on the loose lands, from 30 to 40 acres.
Thirty acres to one horse is, perhaps, a fair average.

	Cotton.	Corn.	Wheat.	Oats.	Rice.	Sweet Potato's.	Hay.	Sorghum.
Average yield per acre,	250 lbs. Lint.	25 bush.	10 bush.	20 bush.	30 bush.	200 bush.	1½ tons.	75 gal.
Cost of produc- tion per acre.	$10	$2.75	$2.80	$2.50	$8.25	$6.00	$5.00	$18.75

The following table of values of lands in the Albemarle
Section is based upon reports of the United States Census, 1880 ; the tax lists of the several counties, and from
responses to letters seeking such information, made by
fifty of the most intelligent and painstaking citizens of
the section, from every county and nearly every part of
the various counties. Any inaccuracies appearing in the
tables are, without doubt, on the side of excessive market
valuation. The actual *average selling* price of cleared
lands in the Albemarle Section throughout does not ex-

ceed $8.00 per acre, and of timber lands $3.50, and it is doubtful if it reaches these figures.

COUNTIES.	Average Asses'd Value Per Acre.			Average Market value per acre.		Average distance from Shipping point.
	All tested lands.	Arable lands.	Timb'r.	Arable.	Timb'r.	
Bertie	3.39	5.00	2.00	8.00	4.00	5 5/6
Camden	2.84	5.00	3.00	12.00	3.00	1 1/2
Chowan	4.78	8.25	2.50	16.75	5.25	2 3/4
Currituck	2.35	8.00	2.75	16.50	8.00	1 1/3
Dare	.73	3.00	.75	7.00	3.50	2 3/4
Hyde	3.38	13.00	3.00	20.87	7.37	2 1/8
Martin	3.14	6.83	2.75	11.25	4.33	4 1/3
Pasquotank	4.62	7.75	3.50	15.50	7.75	4 1/5
Perquimans	4.52	8.25	2.60	13.00	5.00	2 1/4
Tyrrell	1.95	7.25	1.25	10.00	2.80	3 1/2
Washington	3.16	6.00	3.00	13.33	6.66	3 1/6
Average for the Section	3.17	7.12	2.46	13.10	5.25	3

GARDEN TRUCKS.

Though of comparatively recent origin, this industry, under the quickening impulse of adequate shipping facilities provided by the Norfolk Southern Railroad, fairly promises to take rank equally with any agricultural interest in the section. This business is followed to a more or less extent in all the counties of the Albemarle Section, but on a much larger scale in the counties north of the Albemarle Sound, traversed by the railroad. These counties annually produce increasing quantities of early fruits and vegetables and ship them to the great Northern markets. The advantages of soil, climate and proximity to market, by aid of cheap and speedy transportation, put the truck farmer of the Albemarle section in a position to realize all the benefits of these circumstances. No section has superior advantages : few indeed will compare to it. The more southern sections—South Carolina and Florida—have earlier maturing crops, but this is counterbalanced by the increased time and cost of reaching markets with products impaired by transportation. The truck farmer of the Albemarle section offers his products, maturing only a few days later, to the consumer in the Northern cities *the day after they are gathered*, fresh and in good order. Being of the first fruits of the land reaching the markets seasonably, he enjoys all the advantages of prices affected by an unsupplied demand. The maturing season at Norfolk, one of the leading trucking centres of this country, is five or more days later than that of the Albemarle counties. These facts speak volumes. Many farmers throughout this section are to some extent displacing former agricultural staples for the new and more profitable truck crops —crops that yield three, five and not infrequently ten and fifteen dollars clear profit when the old crops yielded one. The trucking industry in the Albemarle country will become permanent, growing and prospering until it becomes a leading feature of its agricultural system, and until north-eastern North Carolina becomes the largest and finest market garden of the great North. It will make the Albemarle farmer more prosperous, and will be one of the prime factors in the erection of the new, enduring prosperity that is beginning to brighten this favored section.

Garden peas, snap beans, onions, cabbage, squash, cucumbers, Irish potatoes, watermelons and strawberries are the chief varieties of truck products raised in this section for shipment to Washington, Baltimore, Philadelphia, New York and Boston.

A few figures supplied by one or two leading farmers will serve the two-fold purpose of showing the value of the industry and the profits realized.

Mr. C. W. Hollowell, near Elizabeth City, Pasquotank County, a leading farmer of the Albemarle section, planted about the first of February, on six acres of land, twelve barrels of Irish potatoes at a cost as follows :

For seed		$30
" ten bags fertilizer		50
" 500 bush. Cotton seed		50
" planting		15
" cultivating		8
" 200 barrels and covers		50
" digging and shipping		20

Total cost of first crop..$223
The yield for this crop was 200 barrels, which sold in Philadelphia
    for $2.75 per barrel net (a low price)...................... $550
Net profit from first crop..................................$327

                                                      $550 $550

At the last of July, on the same ground, he planted a second crop
    of potatoes at the following cost:

For seed		$12
" planting		12
" cultivating		6
" digging		12

Total cost of second crop.................................... $42
This crop yielded 537 bushels, sold for seed for................ $537
Net profit of second crop..................................$495

                                                      $537 $537

Total cost first crop	$223		
Total cost second crop	42	$265	
Total receipts first crop	$550		
Total receipts second crop	537		$1,087
Profit first crop	327		
Profit second crop	495	$822	
		$1,087	$1,087
Profit per acre	$137		

It will be noticed with interest that the profit in the second crop of potatoes was $168 greater than that on the first crop, or $28 greater per acre. Yet comparatively few of our farmers have learned the value of double-crop farming. This year Mr. Hollowell will make three crops of potatoes on the same land. In 1882 he sold his crop in the field for $5.00 per barrel. The same gentleman raised on thirty acres of land 1,100 barrels of Irish potatoes, 800 bushels sweet potatoes, 400 bushels corn, 100 bushels peas, 3,000 pounds fodder, 8 tons millet hay and 75 gallons sorghum syrup, netting him over $100 an acre. He presents this as a fair annual product, and says that with good cultivation it can be done almost any year.

Mr. A. A. Perry, near Edenton, Chowan County, raised this year from twenty-six acres of land, in garden peas, 1,090 boxes of five bushels per box, which netted him $1,970. Upon the same lands he has now crops of cotton, and peanuts that will produce—the cotton about a bale per acre, the peanuts from 100 to 120 bushels. Apportioning the land equally between the two crops, we have a result illustrating at once the profit of trucks and the benefit of rotating crops.

Net profit on peas, ...	$1,970
Value 10 bales cotton, . .	500
" 1,000 bushels peanuts, . . .	1,500
	$3,970

With the most liberal allowance for cost of making the two crops and marketing the second crop, Mr. Perry will make over $100 an acre on his land. He has a small field of five acres which has already netted him $229 from Irish potatoes (in a bad year) and on which corn is now growing that will yield sixty bushels per acre, or 300 bushels for the field, worth $200. These figures are presented not to mean that any farmer, on any land, with any sort of farming, can make $100 per acre, as Mr. Hollowell, Mr. Perry and others have done and are doing. They are only intended to show the value of truck as a money crop in the Albemarle section, and to illustrate the advantages of farming by approved methods. Yet it may be said without exaggeration that in this section thousands upon thousands of acres of land can be bought at a very low figure, just as good naturally, and with care can be made to yield just as much as Mr. Hollowell's or Mr. Perry's.

FISHERIES.

The fisheries of North Carolina are the most important on the South Atlantic coast. The shad and herring fisheries are the most extensive and important of any State, and the fisheries of the Albemarle section of North Carolina are larger, and the products more valuable than those of the balance of the State combined. Especially is this true of the seine fisheries. It is estimated that 300,000 yards of seine are operated in the Albemarle Sounds. In addition there are thousands of stake, drift, pound, and other kinds of nets operated in the great sounds and rivers in this section. The largest of the seines are some 2,500 yards in length, about a mile and a half. From end to end of the hauling ropes, when the seine is out, the distance is nearly four miles. The seines are "shot," that is carried out and deposited in the water, by steam flats, and steam power is also used in bringing them to shore with their great loads of fish. Formerly the "shooting" was all done by means of boats manned by from sixteen to twenty-four sturdy oarsmen, but the inventive genius of a citizen of the Albemarle Section opened the way to better and more rapid methods. To Capt. Peter Warren, of Edenton, is due all the credit for that great modern convenience of the large fisheries known as the steam-flat. The varieties of valuable fishes frequenting the waters of the Albemarle Section in great numbers are numerous. Chief among the commercial fishes are herring, shad, rock (striped bass), mullet, blue fish, spanish mackeral, chub, (black bass,) perch, sturgeon, menhaden, trout, spots, hog-fish, croakers, and of the shell fish, oysters and clams. The crab, so abundant in many places, is the arch enemy of the gill netter, having no respect for either the nets or its finny captives, and destroying both with apparently equal relish. Even this Ishmaelite of the waters is sought for profit, being prepared for market at Hampton, Va., and other places on the coast. The herring as he is universally called, in reality an ale-wife, is entitled to the distinction of king of our commercial fishes ; not that his flavor is so fine as of dozens of other varieties, or that he brings even a hundreth part of what other fish sometimes bring, but because he never fails to come, be the season good or bad.

From fifty to a hundred thousand herrings, and often twice that number are frequently taken at a single haul of a large seine in a good season. It is reliably stated that as many as 400,000 herrings have been saved from a single haul of a seine in Albemarle Sound, thousands of fish escaping and being thrown away for want of hand-ling facilities.

Herring are cured in salt and stored in barrels and kegs. Three grades of them are prepared for market— cut, roe and gross. They are also cured by smoking, though on a much smaller scale. The other most valuable species of food fish taken in the Albemarle waters are shad and rock, caught in great numbers in Albemarle Sound and its tributary streams, and to a less extent in the Pamlico Sound and its tributaries. These fish (and others, as perch, chubs, etc.) are packed in ice and shipped fresh. The North Carolina shad command the highest prices because they begin to "run" first and are early on the market. Thus, while the State of Maryland is credited by the census with a slightly larger catch of shad, the price realized for the North Carolina shad is so much greater that the value of the catch is more than double that of the Maryland fishery, because the shad are marketed before fishing begins there. The quantity of shad taken in the waters of this section in a good year is between three and four million of pounds. The shad is a much more timid fish than the herring and not so easily entrapped. At the head of the Albemarle Sound, made fresh by the volume of water from the Roanoke,

Cashie, Chowan and other rivers, is the favorite spawning grounds of the shad, and it is in their passage hither that they are ensnared in the seines and nets all through the sounds and rivers. At Avoca, at the head of Albemarle Sound, is a hatchery for shad furnished with the most approved appliances. It is a State institution, and the work is done under the auspices of the State Board of Agriculture, by Mr. Stephen G. Worth, Superintendent of Fish and Fisheries. Millions of shad fry have been artificially hatched at this station and turned loose in the inland waters of the State. The number placed in the streams tributary to the Albemarle Sound from 1877 to 1880 was 10,963,000 ; in streams tributary to Pamlico Sound, 3,846,000.

The following summary represents the statistical review of these fisheries :

Persons employed..5,274
Fishing Vessels..95
Fishing boats..2,714
Capital dependent on fishing industries....................$506,561
Pounds of sea products taken, including oysters..........11,357,300
Value of same..$280,745
Pounds of river products taken.........................20,892,188
Value of same. $546,950
Total value of products to fishermen......................$827,695

It is not deemed expedient here to take up the several commercial fishes of the Albemarle Section and treat them in detail, nor even to mention all the very many species of the food fishes. Enough has been said to impress the reader with the real importance and magnitude of this industry. It may be well to add that the Albemarle fisheries in 1880 had about quadrupled their product of ten years before, and that there is still plenty of room for all comers. The business has not begun to approach its full development.

The shell fish of these waters, however, merit some mention. There are extensive beds of clams on the banks, and they are taken from their beds in the sand in great numbers ; the demand is largely local, but the volume of export is increasing through shipments to

New York. The oyster interests of this section bid fair at an early day to assume large proportions by the aid of favorable legislation and by proper culture. The Pamlico Sound and its tributaries form a vast natural oyster field that, with improved methods of culture, will supply a large demand.

The whole floor of the sound, covering hundreds of square miles, can readily be converted into productive oyster fields. In many places the natural oyster rock now covers the bottom for miles, and oysters can be gathered in quantities at a cost of about twenty cents and less per bushel. Some of these oysters are of superior size and quality ; in places where they have been artificially planted they compare favorably with the best cultivated products of the Chesapeake Bay.

The statutes of North Carolina restricting the amount of oyster beds to be entered by one man to ten acres, is a restriction upon outside capital from coming in and developing these interests. It is probable the next legislature by remedying this difficulty, will offer inducements for the development of this, one of the most important and valuable of Eastern North Carolina's exhaustless resources.

Several highly prized varieties of turtle and terrapin are to be found in quantities in the waters of the Albemarle Section. Diamond-back terrapins, the most valuable of them all, abound in places and are taken and shipped in considerable quantities.

TRANSPORTATION.

There is no respect, perhaps, in which this territory, so peculiarly qualified by nature to be a pleasant dwelling place, has been more favored than in the facilities provided alike by nature and art by which to go back and forth to the marts of the land.

Broad sounds, winding rivers and deep estuaries intersperse the land traversed by railroads. The numerous steamers and countless sail which navigate these waters, have access through the inlets of the sea, and by canals, to all the ports of the coast. The railroads, with their steamer connections, reach the most remote and secluded places in the section. There is no part nor inhabitant of it, so isolated as to be deprived of the benefits of frequent, speedy, regular and inexpensive commerce with other men and places.

The principal lines traversing the Albemarle section are the Norfolk Southern Railroad, and the steamboats of the same Company, the steamboat lines of the old Dominion Steamship Company and the Roanoke, Norfolk and Baltimore Steamboat Company.

THE NORFOLK SOUTHERN RAILROAD.

This road was built in 1881, from Norfolk, Va., through Elizabeth City and Hertford, to Edenton on the beautiful bay of that name, at the western end of Albemarle Sound—a distance of 74 miles.

It is well built and thoroughly equipped, providing adequate facilities for travel and shipment to a contiguous territory wonderful for its fertility and the abundant diversity of its products.

Stations at short intervals, and numerous private sidings—furnished upon liberal terms to shippers—have diverted to the road the business of the tributary counties from channels through which it flowed for a century ; new lands have been cleared; mills and factories have been established; new industries started and old ones enlarged, and otherwise its impress has been stamped on all the features and values of the section.

Connecting steamers bring to it from the sounds and rivers, fruits and products of the land, fish from the sea, and fowl from the air, which over this road are speedily conveyed by lines radiating from Norfolk, to the markets of Baltimore, Philadelphia, New York and Boston.

The policy of the Company has been to provide the facilities above generally described to the whole section as rapidly as possible, and without reference to immediate return. In addition to its road it has provided steamboats to run between Elizabeth City and the villages and settlements along the rivers and sounds. The Company's steamers, "Mary E. Roberts" and "Martha E. Dickerman," reach all landings on Pasquotank, North, Alligator, Scuppernong and Little Rivers, and thereby extend to these heretofore remote and inaccessible localities all the benefits and advantages of the railroad.

By prompt employment of necessary appliances and terminal facilities it is meeting the demands of all the interests of the section, not alone moving the crops out and merchandize in, but the coal, ice, salt, lime, and the coarser freights for the full development of the region. Not only the lumber manufactured along the road, but the logs themselves, cut beside the road, and brought miles by water to it, is carried to mills at Norfolk. Its ample and suitable equipment permits the running of numerous and fast trains, which, with its superior connections at Norfolk, have largely increased perishable traffic--fish, game, fruits, vegetables, etc. Brought to the road by steamboats from all points in Eastern North Carolina, from the Upper Roanoke River to Cape Lookout, they are in the market stalls of Washington, Baltimore, Philadelphia, New York and Boston in a few hours.

The Old Dominion Steamship Company.

This Company has been a prominent factor in the material development of Eastern North Carolina. For many years its vessels plied between Norfolk and Newberne and Washington through the Albemarle and Chesapeake Canal until the completion of the Norfolk Southern Railroad to Elizabeth City, when connection was made there with the road, thus reducing the time between North Carolina cities and the Northern markets.

The Company's fleet in North Carolina now comprise the following fine steamers:

The "Shenandoah"...A large full powered side-wheel steamer makes semi-weekly trips between Newberne and Elizabeth City.

The "Newberne"......An iron propeller, large and commodious, makes semi-weekly trips between Elizabeth City and Washington, N. C.

The "Beaufort," and

"R. L. Myers".........On Tar River; run on daily schedules between Washington and Tarboro.

The "Washington"...Covers Pamlico River, reaching points in South Creek, Pungo River, Bath, etc.

By the activity of all these steamers, built especially for the business, immense quantities of the products of field, forest, stream and sea, corn, cotton, rice, potatoes and other vegetables, fruits, rosin, turpentine, woods and lumber, fish, oysters and clams are gathered up and transported speedily and cheaply by their connecting rail and steamer routes to the great markets of the country—Norfolk, Baltimore, Washington, Philadelphia, New York and Boston, and through these ports to the great West and foreign ports, drawing back in exchange all kinds of manufactures. The maintenance of these lines serve to connect the towns and business centres of this wide section with the great arteries of commerce; and it is safe to say that no section of the country similarly situated enjoys greater facilities for the safe, speedy and economical transportation of men and materials than does the tide-water section of Eastern North Carolina.

The Company's main line forms the connecting link at Norfolk for New York and the North and East, and its magnificent fleet of powerful iron steamships, with the finest passenger accommodations, make almost daily trips between those points.

THE ROANOKE, NORFOLK AND BALTIMORE STEAMBOAT COMPANY.

The completion of the Norfolk Southern Railroad to Edenton made possible a quick and positive connection between the Roanoke River and Norfolk and Baltimore, and this Steamboat Company stood ready to seize the opportunity whereby its steamers have since enjoyed the principal traffic of the river. Possessed at that time of a number of steamboats, it has since added to its fleet three large, powerful and swift boats, which fully meet all the requirements made upon its equipment. Its service is of two kinds, viz : between river points and the Norfolk Southern Railroad at Edenton daily and semi or tri-weekly, and between Baltimore and the river direct, weekly. In the first line are employed the elegant passenger and freight steamers "Plymouth" and "Hamilton," and on the other route the fine iron steamers "Conoho" and "Meteor," all of them having been designed and built for the service performed by them.

At Williamston, connection is made with the Albemarle and Raleigh Railroad to Tarboro—and at Jamesville with the Washington and Jamesville Railroad to Washington. Both of these roads are efficient feeders of the line, and combined furnish facilities which have developed, in increasing degree each year, all the commercial, agricultural and fishing interests of the Roanoke watershed.

The route from Tarboro and Washington *via* this line is a favorite one of passengers, who find a satisfactory relief from the tedium of travel in the fast and comfortable steamboats, the pleasant ride upon the waters of this historic stream, and the short rail ride from Edenton through fair, broad and cultivated lands to Norfolk.

All the towns reached by this line, Plymouth, Windsor, Janesville, Washington, Williamston, Hamilton, Robersonville, Bethel and Tarboro, display, with peculiar force, the beneficial results of frequent and efficient communication as afforded by this company.

Other transportation facilities are provided by the Albemarle and Chesapeake Canal, having about seven feet of water and locks 220 feet long and 40 feet wide ; and the Dismal Swamp Canal, with locks 100 feet long and 16 feet wide. A number of steamers and other vessels navigate these canals and carry a considerable part of the commerce of the Albemarle section.

The Albemarle Steamboat Company runs a steamboat, the "Chowan," on the Chowan and Blackwater Rivers, between Plymouth and Edenton, N. C., and Franklin, Va., connecting there with the Seaboard and Roanoke Railroad.

GOVERNMENT AND TAXATION.

The government of North Carolina is a pure democracy. It is based upon the will of the people as expressed in the Constitution, an instrument framed by them in their sovereign capacity through delegates appointed for that purpose. The will of the people of this and of each State, when thus expressed, and in conformity to the Constitution of the United States—for the will of the people of each State is subordinate to the collective will of the people of all the States—is the supreme law. The State Constitution thus made is the measure and test of all laws passed by the Legislature, and these laws must stand or fall by their agreement or disagreement with it.

The Constitution is a short instrument but wide in its scope and bearing. It contains a brief statement of the fundamental principles of civil and individual liberty, creates the different departments of government—Executive, Legislative and Judicial—and prescribes the powers of each ; establishes Educational, Charitable and Penal institutions ; directs who shall be liable to duty in militia ; and prescribes the rights of citizenship.

The Legislature enacts laws. The Judiciary passes upon them when a question arises as to their constitutionality, and expounds them when a question is presented as to their meaning. The execution of the law is entrusted to the Executive. The Executive in this State possesses no veto upon the acts of the Legislature. When the law is once made his duty, as that of every other citizen, is obedience in his sphere.

The rights of citizenship is the only point for consideration here ; and these depend upon age, residence and previous citizenship.

A citizen of a foreign country can make himself a citizen here by becoming a resident; declaring before the proper tribunal his purpose to become a citizen ; and taking the prescribed oath of allegiance.

A citizen of any other of the United States becomes a citizen here by changing his residence from that State to this.

All persons who are born and continue to reside within this State are citizens thereof.

The chief privilege of citizenship is suffrage. The Constitution ordains that, "every male person born in the United States, and every male person who has been naturalized, twenty-one years old, or upward, who shall have resided in this State twelve months next preceding the election, and ninety days in the county in which he offers to vote, shall be deemed an elector."

Suffrage here embraces the right to vote for every officer in the State from the governor down to constable. One only exception to this principle exists in this State —that is in the case of Justices of the Peace. These are appointed by the Legislature. Logical consistency was sacrificed in this case to secure what, in the judgment of the Convention, was a point of far higher importance, namely, the sound administration of justice in the county, and the administration of county finances, both of which are under the control of the Justices. In many of the eastern counties the colored population largely predominates. Newly emerged from slavery, and consequently ignorant of the duties of citizenship ; ignorant of the law, and therefore incapable of administering it ; themselves without property and therefore without the judgment necessary to administer the finances of a community ; it was deemed best to repose the power of making magistrates in an another body ; thus guarding those communities against error, whether of ignorance or design, until experience and education should make those colored majorities safe repositories of such power. This provision of the Constitution was inspired by no feeling of enmity toward the colored man ; it was a provision of safety as well for the colored as for the white man. The provision was made impartial in its operation ; it applies to every county in the State, whether the majority be white or black, and the object was secured. No such provision was necessary in the cases of officers elected by general ticket, for there the experience of the white population accustomed to the exercises of citizenship and educated to its responsibilities would counterbalance the inexperience of the colored race.

Citizenship under the Constitution of North Carolina carries with it high and important rights apart from suffrage. It confers a right to an education by the State, such as will qualify the citizen for the duties to be performed. If he be without property it gives him the right to support from the county if incapable of earning it by sickness or old age. If he have property and is overtaken by irremediable misfortune, it exempts from execution personal property to the value of five hundred dollars, and vests in the owner in fee simple the homestead and the dwellings and the buildings used therewith, not exceeding in value one thousand dollars, to be selected by him. The unfortunate have thus a secure refuge in case of disaster in business.

It regulates taxation by providing that the General Assembly levying a tax shall state the object to which it is to be applied, and enjoins that it will be applied to no other purpose. It establishes an equation between the property and the capitation tax by directing that the capitation tax levied on each citizen shall be equal to the tax on property valued at three hundred dollars in cash. The capitation tax is levied on every male inhabitant in the State over twenty-one and under fifty years of age, which shall never exceed two dollars on the head. The effect of this limitation upon the capitation tax restricts the tax on each hundred dollars worth of property to sixty-six and two-thirds cents. It further directs that the amount levied for county purposes shall not exceed the double of the State tax, except for a special purpose and with the approval of the Legislature.

The rate of State tax levied for the present year is twenty-five cents on one hundred dollars, besides twelve and a half cents school tax.

EDUCATION.

The Constitution of North Carolina, adopted in 1776, ordained as a part of the fundamental law, that "schools shall be established for the convenient instruction of youth, with such salaries to the masters, paid by the public, as may enable them to instruct at low prices." As soon as the resources of the State permitted, this provision of the Constitution was carried into effect. Long before the civil war the system of common schools in this State had attained a full development. A fund of two millions of dollars had been accumulated, the income from which was supplemented by annual appropriations. From 1852 to 1861 our educational progress attracted general attention and admiration. This fund was engulfed in the war, and the system had to be built up anew from the very foundation.

The provision for State education under the new Constitution of North Carolina, if not equal to that of some other States, is yet liberal. The Constitution sets apart a large extent of land, and appropriates all moneys arising from certain specified sources, for establishing and maintaining free public schools in the several counties of the State. Further, it directs the appropriation of 75 per cent., at least, of the State and county capitation tax to the same purpose. The moneys from these sources form a permanent fund for education, which cannot be diverted. The legislation of the last few years shows a growing sense of this great interest. That of the session of 1881 was a marked advance on any that had gone before. In addition to the provisions specified above, a tax of twelve and a half cents was levied on every hundred dollars worth of property and credits, and the tax on the poll was correspondingly increased thirty-seven and a half cents in aid of the education fund. The revenue from these sources was reckoned to be fully adequate to keep open the public schools for four months in the year. If the tax thus levied should prove insufficient to maintain one or more schools in each district for the period named, the county commissioners are required to levy annually a special tax to supply the deficiency. The ages for admission to the public school range from six to twenty-one years.

The organization provided for administering the common-school system is sound and judicious. The Constitution provides a State Board of Education, which has full power to legislate in relation to free public schools, and the educational fund of the State. Its legislation is subject, however, to be altered or amended by the General Assembly. A Superintendent of Public Instruction presides over and directs the operations of the whole system.

Corresponding to a State Board and State Superintendent, there is a County Board and County Superintendent. The County Board is charged with the general management of the public schools in their respective counties. The County Superintendent examines applicants for positions as teachers, visits and inspects the public schools, advises with teachers as to methods of instruction and government, and he may, under regulations prescribed, suspend teachers if incompetent or negligent ; his action in the latter case being subject to review by the County Board.

The County Board of Education in each county have authority to establish a teacher's institute in their county, or the Boards of any number of counties may join in establishing one for the several counties so co-operating.

Each county is laid off into school districts, the convenience of each neighborhood being consulted. In each district there is a school committee consisting of three persons. It is the duty of the committee to provide school houses, employ teachers, and give orders for the payment of the sums due for their services, and take at a stated period a census of the children within school age.

The compensation provided for teachers of the first grade is left to the discretion of the committee ; that of teachers of the second grade is twenty-five dollars a month ; that for those of the third grade is fifteen dollars.

The schools for the two races are separate ; the districts the same in territorial limits, or not, according to the convenience of the parties concerned.

The financial arrangements with respect to the chools fund give the most absolute security for its safe custody and proper application. It is collected by the Sheriff and by him paid to the County Treasurer. It is drawn by a written order of the district committee, which order is countersigned by the County Superintendent. The school fund, it will be seen, is handled by none but bonded officers, and paid out under the most effective checks for its proper disbursement.

For the purpose of training teachers, and thus giving unity to methods of instruction, and the greatest efficiency to its practical working, ten Normal Schools are established—five for the white and five for the colored race—and an equal fund is appropriated to the Normal Schools for each race. Within the last few years graded schools have been established in all the principal towns of the State, and the number is yearly increasing.

The provision for higher education is ample. Private schools for both sexes are numerous. The principal institutions for the education of boys and girls are of the highest order.

At the head of the institutions of learning is the University of the State, an institution established in pursuance of the Constitution, and maintained in part by annual appropriations. Science and learning in their widest range are their taught by professors eminent in their several branches. Second only to the University are the denominational colleges of the State, each having a corps of learned professors and tutors.

RELIGION.

The people of North Carolina are almost entirely Protestant, of various denominations; but all sects are equally free before the law.

THE PEOPLE OF THE SECTION.

Their Character.

In all those things which stamp a high moral impress, no people can look back upon the past with more pride than those of North Carolina. From the foundation of the colony, they have always been noted for those traits of character which give the greatest security to the State, to society and the family. They have always upheld the exercise of constitutional authority; the social duties they have always appreciated and observed; and by none have the domestic ties been more prized and cherished. Industry, frugality and social order have marked every stage of their existence. Yet more, reverence for truth—especially revealed truth—and a sacred regard for business engagements have been ingrained in them.

An observer would be at once struck by the homogeniety of the people, and with the agreeable spectacle of two races living in harmony on the same soil and under the same laws. The first is rare in this age of migration, and particularly in this country, but is easily explained by the natural barriers to commerce which excluded variety of pursuits and made the State essentially an agricultural community. The conservative disposition and tastes which these modes of life nurtured repressed any effort to make known the resources of the State, and to attract settlers. But under the stimulus of our system of railroad transportation which has, in a measure, redressed our natural disadvantages, the new order of things, brought about by the war, and through the necessity of cultivating smaller farms and the consequent

surplus of lands in market, a new spirit has character-
ized the people and turned a general desire toward
immigration.

In regard to the harmony existing between the two
races, Governor Jarvis, in his annual message to the
Legislature, in 1881, said :

"The two races are working together in peace and
harmony, with increasing respect for each other. The
colored population, I am glad to say, are becoming more
industrious and thrifty. Many of them are property
owners and tax-payers. They seem to be learning the
important lesson that they have nothing to rely upon but
their own labor. I have tried, on every opportune occa-
sion, to impress this lesson upon them, and to assure
them of the sympathy and hearty co-operation of the
white race in their efforts to make themselves good and
useful citizens. They have held during the past two
years, in the city of Raleigh, two industrial exhibitions
that were exceedingly creditable to them. I attended
both of these exhibitions, and made short addresses, and
was glad to see that the efforts of the colored race in this
direction found so much favor and encouragement among
the whites. I regard it as an imperative duty from which
the whites cannot escape, if they would, to see that in all
things full and exact justice is done the blacks, and that
they are not left alone to work out their own destiny.
They are entitled, by many binding considerations, to
receive aid and encouragement from the whites, in their
efforts to be better men and women, and I have no doubt
will receive it."

The events of the past two years have confirmed the
justness of this official statement.

The natural increase in our population has been greater
than that from natural and foreign sources in most other
States, and now ranks it as the fifteenth in the number of
its inhabitants in the Union. It increased from 1,071,361
in 1870 to 1,399,750 in 1880, and can now be safely estimated at 1,500,000. Classified by the census according
to sex there were in 1880, 687,908 males, and 711,842
females ; by race, 867,242 whites, 531,267 colored people,

1,230 Indians and one Japanese. The aggregate population consisted of 270,994 families, living in 264,305 dwellings. The number of persons to a square mile was 28.81, the number of families 5.58, dwellings 5.44. The number of acres of land to a person 22.21, to a family 114.73. The number of persons to a dwelling 5.30 ; to a family 5.17.

The percentage of increase from 1870 to 1880 was 30.06 ; of density of population eight per cent.

Distributed according to topography 421,157 of the population live on the South Atlantic coast, 743,739 on the Interior Plateaus and Table Lands ; and 233,654 in the Mountain districts. According to the same distribution 203,771 colored people live on the South Atlantic coast ; 300,236 on the Interior Table Lands ; and 27,270 in the Mountain districts.

THE ALBEMARLE COUNTIES.

BERTIE COUNTY.

Area, 720 square miles; population, 16,401. It is at
the head of Albemarle Sound, and was formed in 1722
from Albemarle County, taking its name from James and
John Bertie, who surrendered their proprietary rights to
the English crown in 1729. The County of Bertie is the
largest in the Albemarle Section. Cotton, corn, potatoes,
peas and native grasses and early vegetables are the agricultural staples. Shingles, staves and fish are largely
exported. The soils are light, loamy and richly alluvial.
Cotton is king in Bertie and holds its sceptre with an
iron grasp, though the introduction of new crops, such
as rice and peanuts, threatens to diminish the kingdom.
No richer lands are to be found anywhere than in Bertie
County, and the advantages offered to the agricultural im-
migrant, with the average assessed value of lands at $3.39
an acre, are not surpassed anywhere. Extensive bodies of
pine, cypress and juniper timber are to be found in the
county, and oaks in smaller quantities; the supply of ash
and the gums is apparently exhaustless. Quantities of
shingles are made in the swamps. Many parts of the
county are especially adapted to fruit culture, apples,
peaches, pears, melons and Scuppernong grapes being
grown extensively. Blackberries, strawberries, whortle-
berries, cranberries and a variety of grapes are among
the indiginous fruits; but the people have yet to learn
to turn these to such profitable account as in other parts
of the State. No county in Eastern North Carolina
possesses better natural facilities for stock raising; as fine

pasturage as there is in the world is found in the marshes or Roanoke bottoms. Luxuriant growth of native grasses spring up everywhere, and there are thousands of acres of reeds that remain green and afford the finest grazing the year around. This land, when cleared, is very productive, but much of it is subject to overflow from freshets in the Roanoke River. It cannot therefore be cultivated in corn or cotton, but it would be impossible to find conditions anywhere more favorable to the cultivation of low land rice. What splendid stock farms and rice plantations they could be made. There are more than fifty miles of available seine ground along the coast of Bertie County ; and on the sound shore several of the largest seines in the world are operated as previously described. Bertie County has no railroad, but its transportation facilities are very good, owing to its extensive water courses. The Roanoke, Norfolk and Baltimore Steamboat Company's steamers and connecting lines reach into the county in almost every direction and brings its products to Edenton for shipment over the Norfolk Southern Railroad. That part of the county along the Chowan River is also well provided with transportation service. There are several small villages in Bertie, Windsor, the county-seat, being the most important.

CAMDEN COUNTY.

Area, 28,009 ; population, 6,274. It was founded in 1777, and named in honor of the Earl of Camden. It lies between the Pasquotank and North rivers. The soil varies considerably, the sandy and dark loams predominating. The surface is as flat as a floor, land fertile and yields well under fair treatment. It is adapted to the grains, grasses, cotton, potatoes, peanuts and trucks. Corn is the leading crop, then cotton and potatoes. Pine, cypress, oaks, gums, juniper, poplar, and maple are among the varieties of valuable timber. The fruits are apples, peaches, pears, and melons, which are grown to a considerable extent. The productions of the county are marketed mainly *via* Norfolk, which they formerly reached through the Dismal Swamp Canal, the southern terminus of which is near South Mills. This slow and uncertain means of transporting perishable goods necessarily checked the development of an industry for which the conditions of soil and climate are favorable. Upon the opening of the railroad this interest became important. At South Mills Dr. F. N. Mullen and others are engaged in the business on a large scale, and the farmers along the line of the railroad are beginning to give it attention, induced by advantages of quick transportation. Through the country, sweet corn, garden peas, Irish potatoes, onions, beans and cabbage are the chief varieties raised. · Camden County has as fine corn land as can be found in North Carolina ; what is locally known as the " Lake," near the line of the railroad, is particularly fertile. One hundred and ten bushels of corn per acre by actual measurement have been raised in this neighborhood without the aid of manure ; while this was an exceptional yield, under favorable conditions, much of this land is capable of producing fifty bushels per acre. It has a rich soil very similar to the famous corn lands of Hyde County.

Sheep raising is something of an industry in Camden, and with good protective legislation, would become successful. In the lower part of the county net fishing is carried on to a considerable extent, though less so than in some of the neighboring counties.

There are two incorporated towns in the county, both creations of the last legislation. South Mills is situated on the Dismal Swamp Canal, about twelve miles northeast of the court-house. It is connected by water with Elizabeth City and Norfolk. The population numbers about 300. It has two churches. two cotton gins. a corn husk factory, a Masonic hall, a flourishing academy, two grist mills, two blacksmith shops, and two stores. Shiloh is in the lower part of the county on the Pasquotank River. Its shipping goes to Elizabeth City by the N. S. R. R. Co's steamer, " M. E. Roberts," whence it is forwarded over the road. The village appears to be thriving and has good trade. Most of its buildings are new.

It may be mentioned as a matter of interest, that a few hundred yards below Shiloh is the site of the first Baptist church built in the State of North Carolina.

CHOWAN COUNTY.

Area, 240 square miles ; population, 7,900. Chowan was one of the original precincts of the Lords Proprietors, taking its name from a tribe of Indians. Along the water courses the soil is mostly a sandy loam, a clay soil in the interior, and in places the dark black soil of the bottoms. All the cereals, hay, potatoes, peanuts, cotton, melons and other trucks, lumber and fish are the staples. Of the field crops cotton and peanuts predominate, more of their staple being cultivated, and the yield, perhaps, larger than in any other county east of the Chowan River. No county in the section has uniformly better lands ; new crops are being constantly added, and the farmers are rapidly learning the new methods of agriculture by which substantial prosperity is to be attained. There are extensive truck farmers around Edenton and in other parts of the county, the annual truck products being large. The introduction of the peanut crop within the past three years marks a new era in the agriculture of this county, the yield being as large as 100 bushels per acre in some localities. The land is specially adapted to grape culture, and quantities of Scuppernong, Concord and other grapes are cultivated for shipment. Other fruits are raised in quantities for market, especially pears. The fishing interests of this county are among the largest connected with this industry, there being about a dozen large seines, some of the largest in the world. The locality is especially favorable to the fisherman from its transportation facilities, by which the principal part of the catch is forwarded by rail from Edenton. Edenton, the county-seat, is the second largest town in the Albemarle section. Population, about 1,500. It is beautifully situated on Edenton Bay, an arm of Albemarle Sound. The town was named in honor of Charles Eden, the Royal Governor of the Province in 1720. It was settled in 1716, and was originally called Queen Anne's Creek, and disputes with one or two others the distinction of being the oldest town in the State. For awhile it was the Colonial Capital and the chief seaport of North Carolina. The Episcopal Church, St. Paul's, the existing records of which bear original date in 1701, was built in 1736, and the court-house fifty years later from brick brought from England. Both buildings are in a good state of preservation. Edenton has about forty stores, two good hotels, a barrel factory, saw mills, several coach and blacksmith shops, four white and three colored churches, an academy and several flourishing private schools, besides public schools for both races. It is the southern terminus of the Nor-folk Southern Railroad and has improved very percep-tibly since that road was built. The steamers of the Roanoke, Norfolk and Baltimore Steamboat Company bring to its wharves large freight from the trans-sound counties for shipment over the railroad, and by means of these steamers direct and speedy communication is had with all points on the Roanoke and Cashie rivers and the surrounding country. A line of steamers up the Chowan and Blackwater rivers connect with the railroad at Franklin, Va.

CURRITUCK COUNTY.

Area, 200 square miles, population, 6,476. This is the extreme north-eastern county of North Carolina. Like the previous county it was one of the original precincts of the Lords Proprietors, and was also named from a tribe of Indians. Between the mainland and the narrow strip of ocean coast is Currituck Sound. The sandy loam soil predominates, though clay loam and other stiff soils are to be found in places. The cereals, cotton, peas, potatoes, melons and other trucks, wild fowl and fish are the chief products. The average of corn and potatoes is larger than of any other field products. Its timbers are pine, cypress, gum, poplar, oak and juniper. The waters of the sounds are stocked with fine food fishes.

There are no large seines in the county, although a

large number of the population are engaged in fishing, set nets and other appliances being used for this purpose. Norfolk is its principal market, being easily accessible over the Norfolk Southern Railroad, which passes through the county from north to south, having three stations within its borders and one just over the northern line, and by one of that Company's Steamer lines from Powells Point, the lower end, to Elizabeth City. Perhaps the most distinctive feature of Currituck, other than agricultural, is its immense game interests. Currituck Sound is a most inviting field for sportsmen. From October to February, it is the resort of millions of ducks, geese, swan and other water fowl. Canvas backs, red heads, black heads, mallard and dozens of other highly prized varieties of ducks are abundant.

Immense "rafts" of these fowl, often miles in length, may be observed in season upon the shallow waters of the Sound, feeding upon the wild celery and many kinds of grasses that cover the bottom. Instances are numerous in which a single gunner has bagged several hundred of these fowl in a day's shooting—several dozen at one shot. The shooting for the main part is done from "blinds," a device of reeds and brush arranged to conceal the sportsman, and "batteries"—a coffin-like boat sunk to the water's edge, with an outside moveable flange at the top to keep the water out. The sportsman thus hid from view, is able to get within gun-shot of the fowl intently engaged in their feeding. "Decoys" are employed to entice the birds within range of the gunner. These decoys are either live fowl anchored to the spot, sometimes trained to call their wild relatives, or wooden images of them. Along the shores of, and on islands in, the Sound are a number of "club houses" owned by Northern sportsmen, who visit the locality to enjoy the shooting every season, reached *via* the Norfolk Southern Railroad at Snowden Station. These clubs own extensive acres of marsh lands, which are favorite resorts of the birds. In acquiring these marshes, erecting club houses, preserving the game, and in shooting it, too, large capital has been invested, which helps to bear the taxation of the county, and employs many persons. The principal clubs are:—

The Currituck,	The Narrows Island,
The Swan Island,	The Palmer Island,
The Lighthouse,	The Monkey Island.

The number of wild fowl killed each year in Currituck Sound by non-resident sportsmen is something enormous. Numbers of residents of the county gain almost their entire livelihood by shooting fowl for the market. No reliable figures can be given of game annually shot in Currituck Sound, and shipped to Norfolk and the northern markets, but the total is large and thousands of dollars come into the county from this source every year. Snipe shooting on the marshes is very fine at certain seasons, and the lower end of the county abounds with deer, bear and other game. Another important industry of this county is trucking. Along the line of the Norfolk Southern Railroad are wide areas of land well adapted to this purpose. Since the completion of the road the business has steadily increased. Peas, cabbage, potatoes and other trucks are raised.

Powells Point, the southern extremity of the county, is well adapted to watermelon culture, it being the staple. The melons are of unusual size, fine quality and mature early, consequently seldom fail to bring the market's best price. Other truck crops are raised in this vicinity, and year by year the acreage is steadily becoming larger.

DARE COUNTY.

Area, 270 square miles. Population, 3,243. The county was formed in 1870 from the counties of Tyrrell, Hyde and Currituck, and named in honor of Virginia Dare, the first white child born on the continent, that event having occurred within its present limits on Roanoke Island, as elsewhere stated.

A greater portion of the lands of Dare County are swampy in the mainland, and pure white sand on the beach. There is some fine land on Roanoke Island, near the mouth of the Alligator River, and on Pamlico Sound.

Corn, peas, potatoes, grasses and vegetables are best suited to these lands. The staples of the county are lumber and fish. There are large bodies of splendid juniper and cypress timber in the swamps ; especially the country tributary to the Alligator River, and a large export timber business is done, very little being manufactured in the county. What has been said of the natural facilities for stock farming in Tyrrell County applies with equal truth to Dare, for the conditions here are precisely similar and the area adapted to the purpose vast.

Everybody in Dare County is either a fisherman or a life-saving serviceman on the beach, and there are 105 so employed out of an adult male population of less than 700.

Fishing, as described elsewhere, is the chief interest of the county, employing four immense seines, as large as any in the Albemarle section. Numbers of small seines, varying in length from 50 to 300 yards, are operated with quantities of stake nets. Oysters, clams, crabs and terrapin abound in great numbers.

The bottom of Pamlico Sound for miles is one vast oyster bed.

Nags Head, a popular resort of eastern North Carolina, is on the banks opposite Roanoke Island. Nature has provided it with advantages for a summer resort possessed by few places on the Atlantic Coast.

It is about forty miles south of Elizabeth City, with which it has connection in summer months by the fine steamers of the Old Dominion line. Other steamers and numbers of sailing craft supply connection with all points of the Albemarle section and beyond.

About five miles from the eastern shore of the mainland of Dare County, and three miles from the beach, is Roanoke Island. It is surrounded by four sounds : Albemarle, Roanoke, Pamlico and Croaton. Manteo, a little hamlet of fifty people, doing a business of $35,000 annually, chiefly in fish, is the county-seat, and is named from the Indian chief who was the first of his race to embrace the Christian religion and receive its ordinances, on the 13th of August, 1584.

HYDE COUNTY.

Area, 430 square miles; population, 7,765. Hyde County was one of the original precincts, and was named in honor of Edward Hyde, who was governor of the colony in 1711. Its eastern and southern shores are indented with great numbers of creeks and bays. The rich, loose, black soil predominates Corn, cotton, wheat, oats, rice, peanuts, lumber and oysters are the staple products. Pine, cypress, juniper, gums, oaks, holly, maple, and nearly all of the other valuable varieties of timber in the Albermarle Section are abundant Almost in the centre of the county is Mattamuskeet Lake, an imposing sheet of fresh water, covering more than 100 square miles.

The predominant feature of Hyde county is its soil and its remarkable growth of corn, which is described by Prof. Ebenezer Emmons, a former State geologist, as follows: "Some tracts have been cultivated over a century, and the crops appear to be equally as good as they were at an early period of their culture, and yet no manure has been employed. and they have been under culture in Indian corn every year, or what would be equivalent thereto. If this crop has been omitted wheat has been substituted for it. not because they are properly wheat soils, but if they are uncultivated the weeds acquire a size that it is impossible to cover them the next year. The same difficulty occurs, in part, in the culture of corn, the stalks are so numerous and large that it is difficult to bury them so completely that they shall be concealed, and preserve at the same time an even, handsome surface. The peculiarities of the soil of Hyde county are comprised in two particulars—

"1st. The large quantity of vegetable matter they contain.

"2d. The extreme fineness of the intermixed earthy matter.

"The earthy matter is invisible, in consequence of its fineness, and is evenly distributed through the mass. An inspection of it, even under a common lens, will deceive most persons, and they would be led to infer that it was entirely absent. Unlike other soils, it contains no coarse visible particles of sand, and hence it appears that during the growth of the vegetables, which cover at least one-half of the soil, it was subjected to frequent overflows of muddy water, or else the area over which these peculiar soils prevail was usually a mirey swamp, which communicated with streams which brought over it the finest sediment of some distant region. This sediment is frequently a fine grit, and fine enough for hones, and when the vegetable is burnt off it appears a light drab color. The character of the Hyde County soil has never been understood ; the cause of their fertility has never been explained, and many persons who are good judges of land have overrated the value of swamp lands, in consequence of the close external resemblance they have borne to those of Hyde. Analysis, however, will, in every case, detect the difference between the common swamp lands and those of Hyde. The color is black or dark-brown, and the whole mass near the surface looks as if it was composed entirely of vegetable matter. We see no particles of sand or soil in it. On the sides and bottoms of the ditches a light grey or ashy soil is discernable. Indeed it is regarded as ashes, and is so called, and is supposed to have been formed by the combustion of ancient beds of vegetable matter.

The cultivated lands of Hyde are not chaffy, that is when dry, like timber, liable to take fire from a spark, or ignited by a gun-wad. There are, it is true, tracts lying in connection with them of this character, which are quite limited, but their occurrence does not affect this general characteristic. It is necessary to dwell further upon the points I have stated respecting the characteristics of these remarkable soils. It will appear in the sequel that there is great uniformity in the composition of these soils, both as regards the amount and condition of the vegetable matter and the quantity and condition of the fine grit intermixed with it.

Regarding as I do these soils as the proper standard for the valuable swamp soils of the eastern section of the

State, I have subjected many samples to a rigid chemical analysis. The results of these analyses have thrown much light over them, and explains satisfactorily their steady productiveness for long periods. It will appear that their fertility is due not only to their vegetable matter, but also to the composition and condition of the earth in combination with it. A number of analyses from tracts which without manure have born a crop of Indian corn for more than one hundred years (as shown by the records of the courts and reliable tradition), none of which show any deterioration by their long cultivation, show that the great supply of nutriment still holds out, and the one hundred years to come, if subjected to no greater drain upon its magazine of food, will, at such a distant period, continue to produce its ten or twelve barrels of corn to the acre. In order to test the value of a soil which has borne a crop for upwards of one hundred years (the ownership and cultivation could be traced back six generations), and during the whole period have not received a bushel of manure, I selected a parcel of it at a distance from buildings, or from a spot which could not have received any artificial aid, and comparing the results of this analysis with soil from adjoining lands that have been under cultivation only three years, it was perceived that all the elements of fertility which belonged to the new and unexhauted soils still belongs to those which have been under cultivation during the last century, and it might be a rich soil at the close of the next century.

The maize must be ranked among the most exhausting crops, and it is evident that poor soils will scarcely repay the farmer for its cultivation. It is evident that unlike other cereals, there is little danger of using too much manure in its cultivation, as it will bear almost any amount without injury, provided all the elements of fertility exist in the magazine of food provided for it While it must be admitted that maize is an exhausting crop, it is equally clear and conclusive that it is one of the most important and valuable, and hence it may be regarded as one that pays best.

The foregoing remarks respecting the maize crop have been made in consequence of the peculiar adaptation of the soil of Hyde County to this cereal. It is the granary of the South. It is true that the number of bushels per acre which constitutes the average crop is less than the number frequently made on other kinds of soils. Thus a hundred bushels of corn may be grown upon an acre, but the Hyde County soils rarely exceed sixty bushels per acre : but from fifty to sixty bushels are grown annually per acre for an indefinite term of years, without the expense of fertilizers, while the heavy premium crops require a great expenditure of them ; and these have to be repeated in order to keep the ground in good condition, and hence, in the long term of years, the profits of those rich lands greatly exceed those which are only moderately so, naturally, and require every few years an installment of manure. "It will be useful in passing," to compare the swamp lands with the prairies of Illinois, on another tract of the great West, whose characteristics have drawn westward so many emigrants from New England, New York and the Old World.

A prairie soil of Illinois is usually black or brownish black, from an intermixture of earthy and sandy matter. It has a basis or subsoil of stiff yellowish clay, and such is the nature of this soil, that it has borne a succession of crops of maize for thirty years, and even more, without manure. These lands are better adapted to maize than wheat, and partly so for the same reasons that this crop succeeds better in all the swamp lands than wheat. Besides, the open prairie lands are swept in the winter by strong chilling winds, which injure wheat by rooting it up. Such influences must bear annually upon lands thus exposed. The crops of corn are larger than in Hyde County, but whether they sell for as much money is quite doubtful.

A prairie crop often reaches a hundred bushels per acre.

The farmers of Hyde seem to be contented with sixty bushels per acre, and at the same time we see no reason why they too might not increase it to one hundred bushels.

Hyde County soils show a greater capacity for endurance than the prairie soils of Illinois, notwithstanding the annual crop is somewhat less per acre. But on the score of location we are unable to see that the Illinois soils have a preference. As it regards health, Hyde County is no more subject to chills and fever than the country of the prairie. It is a remarkable fact that persons live and labor in swamps with impunity or freedom from disease.*

Most varieties of fruit do well in Hyde County, and the delicious Mattamuskeet apple, a native, grows to a perfection not obtained elsewhere. The bottom of Pamlico Sound for the entire length of this county is one of the finest natural oyster fields in the world. In many places it is covered with natural oyster beds, some of which produce oysters of delicate flavor—notably the Far Creek oyster. Hyde County enjoys adequate transportation facilities. The Norfolk Southern Railroad Company's steamer, "M. E. Dickerman," runs between Elizabeth City and Fairfield, on the north side of the county at the head of the Alligator River, and affords ample accommodations for freight and passengers.

The steamers of the Old Dominion and other lines place the southern portion of the county in direct communication with Newberne, Washington, and Elizabeth City. Swan Quarter in the county is a small village situated at the head of Swan Quarter Bay, an arm of Pamlico Sound. Fairfield is a thriving little town on Mattamuskeet Lake; a canal four miles long connects it with Alligator River.

MARTIN COUNTY.

Area, 500 square miles ; population, 13,140.

Martin County was formed in 1774, and named in honor of Josiah Martin, the last Colonial Governor of North Carolina. Much of the soil is a sandy loam ; in many places it is a dark loam with a sub-soil of clay. Rich deposits of blue and yellow marl underlie the surface soil in many places. The staples are cotton, corn, rice,

* Report on the Swamp Lands by Walter Gwinn, 1867.

peanuts, potatoes, lumber and shingles. Cotton is the main crop, and the acreage annually cultivated is larger than any other county of the Albemarle Section, Bertie alone excepted. Cypress, the gums, ash and pine are the most valuable kinds of timber to be found in large quantities. Beech is very abundant along the banks of the Roanoke. The manufacture of shingles by hand and machine, and other lumber is one of the most important industries of the county. Considerable timber is taken outside the limits of the county, and even the State, to be manufactured, notwithstanding there are many large mills in Martin and adjoining counties to be supplied. The condition for stock raising, as described in the sketch of Bertie County, exist quite as favorable in Martin County along the Roanoke.

The territory adjacent to the river is subject to overflow, but the freshets are seldom great enough to do serious damage, and are serviceable in removing shingles and other lumber products from the interior of the swamps. The transportation facilities are all that could be desired, and within the past four years have improved greatly. The Albemarle and Raleigh Railroad traverses the entire county, from the Wilmington and Weldon Railroad at Tarboro to its eastern terminus at Williamston. The steamers of the Roanoke, Norfolk and Baltimore Steamboat Company, plying between this point and Edenton, supply the link which connects this road with the Norfolk Southern Railroad, affording the people of Martin the most direct and quickest route to Norfolk and the North. By this arrangement the people along the Roanoke River are within twelve hours of Norfolk, twenty-four hours of Baltimore and thirty hours of New York. Other steamers of the Roanoke, Norfolk and Baltimore Line ply directly between points on the Roanoke and Norfolk and Baltimore. There are four of them in all, three good sized iron steamers having been added within the past three years.

Williamston, on the Roanoke, is the county-seat of Martin. It has a population of 750 and a large trade.

Twenty miles above by water, on the Roanoke, is the

beautiful prosperous village of Hamilton, with about 500
people, and a trade of near $250,000 per annum. James-
ville on the Roanoke, fifteen miles below Williamston, is
connected with Washington by the Jamesville and
Washington Railroad.

PASQUOTANK COUNTY.

Area, 240 square miles; population, 10,386. The
county was founded in 1729, was one of the original
precincts, and is named from a tribe of Indians. The
land is fertile, yielding well without the use of fertilizers,
and always with a little assistance. Its staples are corn,
cotton, potatoes, wheat, oats, rice, hay, sorghum, truck,
lumber, shingles and fish. As in all the counties of this
belt the soil varies, but is chiefly alluvial and sandy.
Considerable quantity of truck is raised along the line of
the railroad and shipped to the northern markets. In
the northern part of the county are large bodies of valuable juniper, cypress and pine timber, much of which is
now sent to Norfolk to be manufactured. In this section
the lands are specially adapted to the cultivation of corn,
peas and peanuts, and large yields are often obtained;
as much as one hundred and twenty bushels of corn have
been raised on a single acre without manuring. Hay, as
a good money crop, is gaining favor with the farmers,
especially since the highly successful experiment of
raising it for shipment made by the Rev. G. W. Sanderlin on his extensive California plantation, about
eight miles northeast of Elizabeth City, on the line
of the Norfolk Southern Railroad. This hay ranks with
the best Northern article, and three tons to the acre is
not an unusual yield. Between two broad, deep rivers,
with the great Albermarle Sound on its southern shore,
an inland canal to Norfolk, and the Norfolk Southern
Railroad cutting it almost squarely in the middle, Pasquotank County enjoys extraordinary transportation
facilities. The county has recently built at a cost of
$50,000, one of the largest and handsomest court-houses
in North Carolina. Elizabeth City, the county-seat, is

finely situated on the Pasquotank River, and is the largest, and in all respects the most important town in this section. By the census of 1880, it had a population of 2,315. To-day the population is hardly under 4,000, which is an evidence of the benefit of the Norfolk Southern Railroad and its connecting steamer lines. New people have moved in, dozens of stores have been built, the costliest and handsomest in the section ; many residences have been erected, some of the best class. The value of permanent improvements made in this town within the past four years will amount to several hundred thousand dollars ; property of all kind has advanced in value ; the volume of business has expanded, and more general progress has been made than for over twenty-five years previous to this time. Elizabeth City has over a hundred stores, five hotels, one of them as large and handsome as any in the State, two saw and grist mills, two planing mills, a carriage manufactory, a net and twine factory, a cotton seed oil mill, two brick yards, one to press brick, a steam cotton gin, an oyster-packing establishment, five blacksmith shops, a ship yard, three newspapers, three job printing offices, a bank, three livery stables, a theatre. a beer-bottling and soda establishment, a handsome and commodious academy, and a number of private and public schools. a normal school for the colored race, a State normal school for the white race, four churches for whites and two for colored. It has an excellent harbor, and in the centre of trade of a large section of country. The Norfolk Southern Railroad places it in easy reach of all points north and south.

The two steamer lines of this company open up to it a large trade in Hyde, Tyrrell, Dare, Washington, lower Currituck and Camden Counties, and establish direct communication with these communities ; the splendid steamers "Shenandoah" and "Newberne," of the Old Dominion Steamship Line, pile upon its wharves the products of the Neuse and Pamlico sections for shipment over the Norfolk Southern Railroad, the quickest route north : a line of small steamers plies through the Dismal Swamp Canal to Norfolk ; and innumerable sailing craft

connect it with the remotest parts of the large territory
lying on the great sounds and rivers of this section. Two
lines of telegraph, north and south, put it in easy speak-
ing distance with the world. What wonder that with
such a stimulus the town should increase in size 40 per
cent. and in importance fully 100 per cent. in the short
space of four years, and continues to grow and prosper?

Nixonton, a small village on Little River, once the
county-seat, is reached by the Norfolk Southern Railroad
Company's steamer "M. E. Roberts," which takes its
products to Elizabeth City.

PERQUIMANS COUNTY.

Area, 220 square miles. Population, 9,468. This was
the earliest permanent white settlement in North Carolina. It has the same variety and gravitation of soil as
the other counties north of the Albermarle Sound. All
the grains, cotton, hay, potatoes, peanuts, sorghum,
truck and many kinds of fruit are grown to perfection.
There are twelve saw mills and four shingle mills in the
county, and a large amount of lumber and shingles is
annually manufactured. There is more corn raised than
of any other cereal, cotton next, more wheat is grown
here than in any county north of the sound, and of a
superior quality. The soil being well adapted to the cultivation of wheat and oats, of which large quantities
were once raised and can be again when the farms are
restored to proper condition. Timothy grass was first
discovered in the lower part of this county and introduced to the public notice. Beds of marl underlie nearly
this entire county, coming to the surface in many
places where they can be easily worked.

About $20,000 capital is invested in fisheries, which give
employment to about 175 laborers.

Sheep-raising is becoming an important industry, and
the conditions are very favorable to stock-raising. The
Norfolk Southern Railroad runs through the county, and
has five stations in its limits--more than any other county
along the route. Like the other counties forming this
belt, Perquimans has very many advantages in the way

of transportation facilities, and what has been said of
them relative to the impetus thus given to trade, may be
as truly said of it. The culture of Scuppernong grapes,
especially in the northern part of this county, is a new
and profitable industry. Last year one thousand barrels
of these grapes were shipped to northern markets from
the immediate vicinity of Belvidere. As an illustration
of the value of these lands for trucking purposes, it may
be mentioned that from a two-acre lot at Hertford a crop
of snap beans has been marketed this year at a clear
profit of one hundred dollars. Twenty-five dollars worth
of apples were sold from the same lot, besides two barrels
of vinegar made and a quantity of fruit wasted. The
same land is now in cotton, with every indication of a
good yield, which will bring the total clear profit from
the two acres to more than two hundred dollars. Yet
there are hundreds of acres of land in the county to be
bought for ten dollars or less per acre, that can easily be
made to do as well.

Hertford is the chief town of Perquimans, and the
county-seat. It is situated on Perquimans River, about
twenty miles from its mouth, the whole distance being
navigable for vessels of large size. It is a town of about
800 population, with a land-tax valuation of $75,000. The
market value of this property is perhaps double that sum.

There are twelve retail stores doing a business of more
than $200,000 annually ; two coach shops, two blacksmith
shops, three churches for the white race and two for the
colored, a large and beautiful academy, one white public
school and one colored, a telegraph line, a steamer line
to points on the Perquimans River and Norfolk, and rail
connections north and south.

TYRRELL COUNTY.

Tyrrell County bears the name of John Tyrrell, one of
the original owners of the province, and lies between the
Scuppernong and Alligator rivers. A large preponderance of the lands of this county remain uncleared ; they
are level, requiring drainage. When properly drained
they are not surpassed in productiveness by the best
lands in the section. Cotton, corn, rice and potatoes are

the chief products; the other staples are lumber, shingles and fish. Immense tracts of valuable timber are to be found in this county, and millions of feet are cut annually. The varieties most abundant and most worked are cypress and juniper, which is transportep outside of the State to be manufactured, and millions of shingles are made every year, the timber business employing a large capital and hundreds of laborers. Much of the county is adapted to stock raising, and this business is conducted more largely than in any other county of the Albemarle Section. The cattle are allowed to run wild in the swamps, feeding on rich growth or reeds always fresh and green. No attention whatever is paid them but to mark the young stock and to hunt down the animals like other wild beast when wanted. Thousands of wild cattle thus roam the swamps at large, never coming out to the cleared land except when pinched with hunger in severely cold weather. There is no organized system of stock farming in Tyrrell County,though a number of men own herds numbering hundreds. Extensive bodies of this land are still held by the State; they could be entered at trifling cost and converted into as fine stock ranches as exist in the world. They could be enclosed, too, with wire fencing at an inconsiderable cost, and under intelligent management the business would yield a handsome profit. Not only reeds and native grasses for the cattle are superabundant, but a variety of native roots and nuts that make the best of food for hogs. Of these a kind of wild "chufa" and "tuckahoe" root are the most prized. Hogs live on them and require no other food, except in winter season. No section has superior advantages for raising bees, and nowhere are they to be found in greater quantities than in the southern part of Tyrrell County. None of the approved appliances for bee culture are used here. When it is desired to take the honey the entire hive is condemned to death. They are worth about $2.00 a stand and will yield$4.50 annually in honey and wax, besides the natural increase of one and one-half swarms per hive. Formerly there were operated along the shores of Tyrrell County some of the largest seine fisheries on the Sound; but they were destroyed in the late war, and for want of capital have never been refitted. The fishing operations now are conducted chiefly by Dutch and set nets, of which there are a great number. The product of these fisheries are very large.

Tyrrell County has very good transportation facilities. One of the Norfolk Southern Railroad Company's steamers, "M. E. Roberts," runs from landings on the Scuppernong River to Elizabeth City; another of the Company's steamers, "M. E. Dickerman," offers adequate service to the people of the Little and Big Alligator rivers. Both connect at Elizabeth City with the railroad.

Columbia, the county-seat of Tyrrell, is well situated on the Scuppernong River. It has a population of about 200, and a good local trade from the surrounding country.

WASHINGTON COUNTY.

Area, 350 square miles ; population, 8,928.

The county was formed in 1779 from Tyrrell County. Its staples are cotton, corn, rice, lumber and fish. All the small grains, hay, peanuts, potatoes and truck are grown. The soil varies greatly, with a preponderance, perhaps, of the sandy loam peculiar to all the counties of the Albemarle section. Cypress, juniper, pine, the gums, poplar, ash and maple are the most valuable timbers, though nearly all the timbers known to this section grow here. There are no large seines in the county, but quite a number of Dutch nets and stake nets, which take fish in considerable quantities.

Trucking is quite an important industry in some parts of the county, especially in the vicinity of Plymouth. Shingles and lumber are largely manufactured. Some of the land is well adapted to fruits.

The lands of Washington County are generally productive, and yield bountifully without the use of fertilizers. Especially is this the case in the vicinity of Lake Scuppernong, a beautiful island basin of fresh water, nine miles long by seven wide. The surface of this lake is several feet above the level of the sound. Great canals lead to it from the splendid farms bordering upon it. The soil here is a black, vegetable loam, of precisely the nature of the fine corn land of Hyde County. Forty and fifty bushels of corn per acre are often obtained.

"The culture of rice, as now pursued in this State, demands express notice. Though the crop has been a staple in North Carolina since its early existence as a colony, the awakened spirit of enterprise among our people has transferred to and domesticated it in counties and sections of the State where it was never cultivated before. It may thus take its place among new industries. This crop presents a singular instance of the revolutions which are accomplished by the break up of old systems of industry and the introduction of new systems. Before the termination of the war, the valley of the Cape Fear possessed a monopoly of this crop in this State. That event broke up the old system of labor, and broke down the culture of this crop there. It was long supposed it could be grown only under the peculiar conditions to be there found. But during the war rice was furnished as an article of food to troops, and it was an article of food generally accessible to the people. These circumstances combined led to general experiments in its cultivation, and these experiments proved it could be grown upon low-lying lands, up to the foot of the mountain range. The introduction of upland rice gave a still further impetus to its cultivation. This new industry— new because under conditions so different from those existing before—has now become an established and a most important one. It has become a staple crop in counties where none was produced a few years ago. The county of Hyde alone produces now, if such statistics as are accessible to us may be trusted, nearly as much rice as the entire Cape Fear valley produced before the war."

It is grown probably to some extent in each of the Albemarle counties, but it is one of the principal products of this county, and is successfully cultivated in the rich soils about the lake, the waters of which, through the canals leading from it, can be utilized for inundation.

Rice culture has been for some years intelligently and extensively prosecuted by Mr. C. L. Pettigrew, upon his several plantations in the county ; by his neighbor,

Mr. Arthur Collins, and also upon the adjoining plantation owned by Mr. H. H. Page, of Edenton.*

These lands have been constantly in cultivation for years and years, and appear to be inexhaustible. Much fine land in this section is covered with a small wooded growth, and could be readily cleared and cultivated.

Washington County is by no means lacking in the important respects of ample transportation facilities.

The Norfolk Southern Railroad Company's Steamer, "M. E. Roberts," brings the products of the rich Scuppernong Section to Elizabeth City for shipment over the the road ; another runs direct to Norfolk. Steamers leave Plymouth regularly for points in the surrounding country, and direct for Norfolk and Baltimore. Daily connection is made by steamers from Plymouth with the Norfolk Southern Railroad at Edenton, the most direct and quickest route to Norfolk and beyond.

Plymouth is the county-seat of Washington and one of the most important towns in this section. It has a population of 1,500 and does an immense mercantile retail business. It has many large stores, several hotels and ample church and school facilities. Among the more important industries is the Plymouth Iron Works, the only establishment of the kind in eastern North Carolina. This institution does a flourishing business. Considerable historic importance attaches to Plymouth on account of the part it took in the late civil war. Three times was it in the scene of conflict. First, was its attack and capture by the Confederates (Col. Wm. F. Martin's 17th N. C. Reg.), under Lt. Col. John Lamb, Dec. 10th, 1862 ; second, the memorable battle of Plymouth, lasting over three days, April 2d, 1864, between the Union forces under Gen'l Wessels and Lt. Flusser of the Navy, and the Confederate Genl's R. F. Hoke, and M. W. Ransom, and the Confederate iron clad "Albemarle," which ended with the capture of Plymouth by the Confederates, and with it Genl. Wessels and 2,200 prisoners.

The U. S. steamers, Southfield and Miami, were sunk and many lives lost ; the Confederates lost heavily during the assault. Third, the re-capture of the town and distruction of the "Albemarle" by Lt. Cushing, U. S. Navy, in October, 1864.

APPENDIX.

—..

The following tables, compiled from the Compendium of the U. S. Census, 1880, were prepared with reference to the North Carolina State Exposition of 1884, at a time when it was supposed that two counties—Gates and Hertford—included in the table but not in the descriptive pamphlet—would unite with the Albemarle Counties in their exhibit.

As the information pertaining to those counties is valuable, it has been retained in the tables.

AGGREGATE POPULATION OF THE THIRTEEN ALBEMARLE COUNTIES, NORTH CAROLINA,

As shown by United States Census 1860, 1870 and 1880,

Showing Increase or Decrease and Percentage of each County to State Population end each period.

No.	COUNTY	1860.		1870.			1980.			REMARKS.
		Population.	Per cent. of State Population.	Population.	Per cent. of State Population.	Increase or Decrease since 1860.	Population.	Per cent. of State Population.	Increase or Decrease since 1870.	
1	Bertie	14,310	.0144	12,950	.0121	360 D	16,399	.0118	3,449 I	
2	Camden	5,343	.0053	5,361	.0050	18 I	6,274	.0045	913 I	
3	Chowan	6,842	.0069	6,450	.0060	392 D	7,900	.0056	1,450 I	State Population.
4	Currituck	7,415	.0075	5,131	.0048	2,284 D	6,476	.0046	1,345 I	
5	Dare			2,778	.0026	2,778 I	3,243	.0023	465 I	Census, 1860, 992,622
6	Gates	8,443	.0085	7,724	.0072	719 D	8,897	.0063	1,173 I	" 1870, 1,071,361
7	Hyde	7,732	.0079	6,445	.0060	1,287 D	7,765	.0055	1,320 I	" 1880, 1,399,750
8	Hertford	9,504	.0095	9,273	.0086	231 D	11,843	.0085	2,570 I	
9	Martin	10,195	.0103	9,647	.0090	548 D	13,140	.0094	3,493 I	
10	Pasquotank	8,940	.0090	9,131	.0076	809 D	10,369	.0074	2,238 I	
11	Perquimans	7,238	.0073	7,945	.0074	707 I	9,466	.0067	1,521 I	
12	Tyrrell	4,944	.0050	4,173	.0039	871 D	4,545	.0032	372 I	
13	Washington	6,357	.0064	6,516	.0060	159 I	8,928	.0064	2,412 I	
		97,263	.0970	92,524	.0864	4,839 D	115,245	.0830	22,721 I	

POPULATION BY RACE OF THIRTEEN ALBEMARLE COUNTIES..

NORTH CAROLINA, CENSUS 1880.

COUNTIES.	WHITE.	COLORED.
Bertie	6,815	9,584
Camden	3,791	2,483
Chowan	3,633	4,267
Currituck	4,495	1,981
Dare	2,875	368
Gates	4,973	3,924
Hyde	4,424	3,341
Hertford	5,122	6,721
Martin	6,661	6,479
Pasquotank	4,855	5,514
Perquimans	4,795	4,671
Tyrrell	3,110	1,435
Washington	4,554	4,374
	60,103	55,142

ASSESSED VALUATION AND TAXATION, ALBEMARLE COUNTIES.

NORTH CAROLINA, 1880.

COUNTIES.	ASSESSED VALUATION.			TAXATION.			
	REAL ESTATE.	PERSONAL PROPERTY.	TOTAL.	STATE.	COUNTY.	CITY, TOWN AND VIL'GE.	TOTAL.
Bertie	$1,202,097	$533,131	$1,735,228	$7,739	$7,811	$450	$16,000
Camden	363,439	149,405	512,844	2,513	5,861		8,374
Chowan	579,101	238,809	817,910	3,715	5,550	1,400	10,665
Currituck	327,592	190,113	517,705	2,192	3,026		5,218
Dare	111,507	98,577	210,084	40	2,507		3,647
Gates	456,345	333,423	789,768	3,502			6,804
Hyde	397,285	288,620	685,905	4,001	6,438		10,439
Hertford	848,875	441,843	1,290,718	5,468	8,440	350	14,258
Martin	952,639	478,554	1,431,193	7,194	6,287	225	13,706
Pasquotank'.	863,662	308,438	1,172,100	6,362	13,260	2,200	21,822
Perquimans.	720,533	301,510	1,022,043	5,701	9,519	260	15,480
Tyrrell	222,629	169,986	392,615	1,695	2,025	7,000	3,791
Washington.	453,479	210,393	663,872	3,689	3,536	280	7,505
	$7,499,183	$3,742,802	$11,241,985	$54,911	$77,562	$5,236	$137,709

FARM AREAS AND VALUES, 1880, ALBEMARLE COUNTIES, NORTH CAROLINA.

COUNTIES.	Farms.	Improved Land.	Value of Farms, including land, fences, and buildings.	Value Farming Implements and Machinery.	Value Live Stock.	Cost building and repair Fences, 1879.	Cost Fertilizers purchased, 1879.	Estimated Value of all Farm Products (sold, consumed, or on hand) for 1879.
	No.	Acres.	Dollars.	Dollars.	Dollars.	Dollars.	Dollars.	Dollars.
Bertie	1,762	85,504	1,327,836	56,326	236,304	20,611	29,583	718,151
Camden	761	36,757	994,650	28,587	123,085	7,910	3,064	267,978
Chowan	716	36,052	607,909	23,262	76,176	9,456	5,043	241,785
Currituck	814	41,170	720,031	17,624	101,310	4,760	4,342	193,457
Dare	193	2,553	105,156	4,431	29,698	2,072	241	19,031
Gates	1,191	49,084	745,114	34,171	123,443	14,088	9,330	260,969
Hyde	789	32,153	1,019,621	27,331	97,915	10,050	1,743	173,079
Hertford	1,128	55,857	1,265,975	49,501	166,242	20,454	32,636	542,608
Martin	1,308	57,030	980,005	46,752	163,806	23,897	22,714	517,102
Pasquotank	919	51,770	1,011,145	47,619	124,890	29,317	2,817	292,227
Perquimans	1,016	54,433	1,123,927	39,187	160,696	17,599	3,696	376,913
Tyrrell	567	19,801	351,495	19,828	68,796	4,992	4,042	132,257
Washington	964	31,695	679,147	45,258	127,035	13,838	12,169	347,188
	12,188	555,759	10,942,011	439,877	1,599,396	179,044	131,420	4,082,745

PRINCIPAL VEGETABLE PRODUCTIONS OF THIRTEEN ALBEMARLE COUNTIES, NORTH CAROLINA, 1880.

COUNTIES.	CEREALS.					VALUE OF ORCHARD PRODUCTS.	HAY.	RICE.	COTTON.	POTATOES.		TOBACCO.
	BARLEY.	WHEAT.	Indian Corn.	OATS.	RYE.					IRISH.	SWEET.	
	Bushels.	Bushels.	Bushels.	Bushels.	Bushels.	Dollars.	Tons.	Pounds.	Bales.	Bushels.	Bushels.	Pounds.
Bertie		2,169	345,091	20,517	191	6,577	35	16,861	7,290	5,699	94,473	554
Camden		4,428	293,447	8,854	30	2,061	108		823	14,812	26,823	
Chowan		4,357	143,156	6,488		984	68		2,223	4,189	62,247	398
Currituck		892	374,819	2,734	75	733		7,727	139	6,702	42,502	
Dare		167	11,205	230		1,119	10	2,780	8	1,996	19,717	
Gates		4,187	170,612	10,016	133	1,979	128		1,863	1,294	87,494	620
Hyde		8,949	243,623	18,400	334	1,818	6	304,671	718	1,594	20,236	517
Hertford		6,891	236,038	14,512	151	2,783	75		6,360	4,282	76,439	2,160
Martin		6,254	227,415	11,229	98	1,694	21	3,150	6,383	3,039	92,913	211
Pasquotank		22,453	348,119	17,438	259	2,053	62	276,174	2,226	3,463	65,807	1,520
Perquimans		25,514	292,850	13,921	380	1,559	152	2,090	2,778	7,921	99,498	400
Tyrrell		2,067	108,839	7,622		591		237,315	1,123	1,703	31,739	
Washington	50	5,564	217,631	13,427		2,905	5	60,873	3,524	3,711	48,429	685
TOTAL	50	93,912	2,964,955	145,788	1651	26,856	970	911,841	33,458	56,305	768,717	7,065

LIVE STOCK AND ITS PRODUCTIONS OF THIRTEEN ALBEMARLE COUNTIES, NORTH CAROLINA, 1880.

COUNTIES.	LIVE STOCK.							WOOL.	DAIRY PRODUCTS.		
	Horses. No.	Mules and Asses. No.	Work Oxen. No.	Milch Cows. No.	Other Cattle. No.	Sheep. No.	Swine. No.	Pounds.	Milk. Gallons.	Butter. Pounds.	Cheese. Pounds.
Bertie	1,517	948	845	2,595	5,559	4,001	33,572	10,087	10	11,745	20
Camden	885	298	145	1,054	1,717	1,273	10,255	5,061		18,758	205
Chowan	653	385	163	736	1,495	375	8,475	1,172	1,539	5,960	
Currituck	1,036	188	182	1,241	2,315	1,764	10,797	5,147		2,995	61
Dare	351	24	125	421	1,217	797	2,243	1,778	10	5,627	
Gates	1,041	294	531	1,456	3,810	2,225	13,072	6,573	200	12,169	122
Hyde	853	217	485	1,547	3,128	1,313	8,642	3,896		21,109	190
Hertford	1,158	557	637	1,323	2,504	1,918	12,010	4,069		8,001	170
Martin	878	879	387	1,653	3,199	2,230	15,808	4,238	10	11,954	
Pasquotank	8 4	421	473	1,094	2,218	813	9,063	2,401	1,438	21,712	211
Perquimans	983	537	460	1,489	3,224	1,747	10,398	7,020	65	25,413	
Tyrrell	316	266	209	1,083	2,597	1,437	6,124	4,038	2	9,169	
Washington	660	418	259	1,329	2,355	746	8,878	2,299	559	14,834	
	11,165	5,432	5,901	17,024	35,538	20,639	149,367	57,779	3,833	169,446	979

THE ALBEMARLE EXHIBIT.

This pamphlet has been prepared for distribution through the medium of the North Carolina State Exposition, and the Exhibit of the Section which it describes.

That Exhibit does not, however, fully and properly represent the Section. For reasons not to be explained within the limit of this paragraph, the work of its collection and preparation did not begin until late in July, when an Agent was selected to collect and display the Exhibit. The difficulty of canvassing eleven counties, and collecting and preparing information, in the time allotted, may readily be imagined.

The season for obtaining many representative products of the Albemarle Section had passed before the work of preparation was assigned to an Agent; notably fish, water fowl, sheaf grains and most of the fruits—of which, therefore, a partial display only is possible. Three-fourths of the timber shown has been procured since September 1st, and no attempt was made to prepare fruits in any form before September 15th.

The hope is expressed that, in passing judgment on the Albemarle Exhibit, the public will take these facts into consideration.

F. E. V.

.

www.ingramcontent.com/pod-product-compliance
Lightning Source LLC
Chambersburg PA
CBHW020326090426
42735CB00009B/1427